OREGON ROAD TRIPS

COLUMBIA RIVER GORGE EDITION

Discover the Gorge!
Mike & Kristy

MIKE & KRISTY WESTBY

"Good roads are more than my hobby, they are my religion."

Sam Hill - Builder of the "King of Roads", the Columbia River Highway

FOLLOW
DISCOVER-OREGON

The Columbia River Gorge

On the Web:
www.Discover-Oregon.com

On Twitter:
@DiscoverOre.com

On Facebook:
www.Facebook.com/DiscoverORE

On Instagram:
DiscoverOregon4300

OREGON ROAD TRIPS - COLUMBIA RIVER GORGE

Discover The Columbia River Gorge

An adventurous 5-day road trip exploring the Columbia River Gorge is now as easy as 1-2-3...

1) Write in the Dates of Your Trip
2) Make Your Historic Hotel Reservations
3) Pack Your Bags and Go!

Using this easy-to-use guide, you'll simply turn each page as you motor along and choose which points of interest to stop at and explore during your day's journey, *all while making your way toward an evening's stay at a historic Oregon hotel.*

Your Journey

INTRODUCTION

Multnomah Falls – Columbia River Gorge

Oregon is a vast and beautiful state. I could list its square mileage, its demographics or perhaps the distance from border to border, but a better description is...it starts with the shores of the Pacific Ocean on its western edge, traverses east over the Oregon Coast Range and into the verdant Willamette Valley, climbs over the snowy summits of the Cascade mountain range while skirting south of the sublime Columbia River Gorge and then continues forever into the remote, silent and dramatic beauty and history of far eastern Oregon.

This guide is about setting out on your own adventure to explore the majestic Columbia River Gorge. It's about the journey, not the destination. It's about asking, "I wonder what that is?" Opening a door and saying "Hello". Shutting off the engine and listening to the never-ceasing sound of a towering waterfall as its torrents drop with both power and grace. It's about trying to comprehend the mighty Columbia River, wondering just how many stars a sky can hold, and what would really happen, I mean *really* happen, if you just kept going.

How To Begin

The Columbia River Gorge's immense size, historical treasures and abundance of geological features can be too much to capture in one trip. In fact, its countless riches can be so intimidating that travelers don't know where to begin...so they don't. Analysis paralysis.

Good news! This book already has your route planned for you. There are only three simple things you need to do...

1) Select the 5-day period for your trip and write those dates into this book at the beginning of each chapter.

2) Call and make reservations at the historic hotels found at the end of each day, which correspond with your chosen dates.

3) Pack your bags, hop in the car and simply choose the sights you wish to stop at and explore each day as you motor along. It's that easy!

Note that some of the optional activities you'll enjoy during your trip, such as flying in a historic biplane or riding aboard a sternwheeler, will also require reservations, and these are noted at the beginning of each chapter/day.

Timing

Your Columbia River Gorge road trip is a beautiful journey most anytime of the year, with the conditions changing dramatically from season to season. Spring, summer and fall in "the Gorge" bring some of the finest weather in Oregon, as well as the entire United States, while winter can bring sunny mornings embraced by cool temperatures and wispy fog...or, quite often, treacherous icy conditions that can lock down travel for days. You'll want to be sure to check the weather forecast before leaving on your road trip.

Wildflowers in the Springtime

If it is springtime and you like wildflowers, then you want to be in the Gorge. Lupine, Chocolate Orchids, Penstemon, Indian Paintbrush, Howell's Daisy, Shooting Stars, Columbines and many others, including the dramatic Arrowleaf Balsamroot, cover the hillsides in an abundance of color. The wildflowers of the Columbia River Gorge do not bloom all at once, but instead over a period of about four months, usually mid-February through mid-June, with April and May offering the most vibrant displays. You'll find most of the wildflowers from the mid-gorge to out east, with locations such as Rowena Crest, Catherine Creek (Page 108), Coyote Wall, the Dalles Mountain Ranch, the Mosier Plateau (Page 74) and many other sites offering outstanding experiences. While we list a couple of convenient wildflower spots in this guide, there are many more that are available with the aid of a short or long hike. If you are planning on visiting the gorge in the springtime, especially during April and May, we highly recommend you do an online search to learn more about the colorful Columbia River Gorge wildflowers.

The Colors of Autumn

Every fall, the deciduous trees of the Columbia River Gorge paint a scene of striking fall colors. The hillsides become accented with yellows, oranges, and vibrant reds as the leaves of Birches, Aspens, Willows, Poplars, and Big Leaf Maples bid adieu to summer in a brilliant performance of autumn colors. It's Oregon's version of New England's fall colors, and you won't want to miss it if you are traveling here in late September and October.

Poison Oak
(& Ticks and Snakes)

"Leaves of three, let it be!"

Don't let this stop you from enjoying a hike during your road trip, but be *very* mindful of poison oak when hiking in the Gorge, especially in the wooded areas at the eastern end. Just because you're on vacation doesn't mean it's taking a break from what it does best, and that is to cause a very itchy, blistering rash. Its deep green leaves cluster in groups of three, and the plant itself typically grows up to a few feet off the ground, so be mindful of small children, as it is right at their height. Its shiny leaves can be tempting for a child to grasp, but that shine is the oil that causes the rash, so don't touch it or brush against it with your clothes. Note that symptoms of a rash can take 12 hours to 10 days to appear.

In addition to Poison Oak, keep an eye out for ticks, especially if you have a dog, as well as any snakes. Most are harmless, but the rocky terrain of the eastern Gorge can harbor rattlesnakes, and these are highly venomous.

WHERE TO START

The "official" first stop of your 5-day road trip is in Troutdale, Oregon, at the western edge of the Columbia River Gorge.

ADD OR REMOVE A DAY TO CUSTOMIZE YOUR TRIP

This 5-day road trip of the Columbia River Gorge can actually be any length you'd like. To shorten your trip, simply skip a night or two and combine the activities of a couple of days together. Want to lengthen your trip? Then by all means book another night at what will soon be your favorite new historic hotel and enjoy a leisurely extra day in your travels.

VISIT MT. HOOD

If you've never been to majestic Mt. Hood, but you've always wanted to see it up close, then this road trip may be your opportunity, especially since you're "in the neighborhood." See Page 132 for information on how to add one day to your road trip so as to journey from Hood River, OR or Dufur, OR up to Timberline Lodge at 6,000' on Mt. Hood. Want to take a road trip around Mt. Hood? Then see our book, *Oregon Road Trips – Mt. Hood Edition.* You can learn more about it on Page 138.

SOME GROUND RULES

325. COLUMBIA GORGE LOOKING EAST FROM CROWN POINT, COLUMBIA RIVER HIGHWAY, OREGON.

"It's the Journey, Not the Destination."

The key to your journey is to alter your driving mindset. It really isn't about getting *there*, it's about discovering *here*. With this in mind, here are some ground rules to follow...

- Get used to stopping the car and getting out.
- Now stop the car and get out.
- Stop the car and get out...again. You'll be glad you did.
- Always ask "I wonder where that goes?"...and go there.
- Hit the brakes and turn right.
- Open the door and say "Hello."
- Don't assume it has to be a short conversation.
- Never mind that you just stopped back there...stop again here.
- Yes, it is a nice view. Feel free to stop, get out and admire it.
- This very moment is the time to do it. You won't be coming back this way next week.
- Enjoy the journey!

Travel Beyond the Page

By all means, do not feel you have to stop at only the places found in this book, as there are many more than those listed here just waiting to be discovered. Go ahead...follow that narrow lane, stop at that small museum, walk the trail to the viewpoint, and open the door to the shop that looks closed, but isn't. It's all about taking the time to...discover Oregon.

The Same, But Different

Following the information in this guide, you will enjoy a unique and exciting vacation discovering the Columbia River Gorge. It's important to note, however, that with a little creativity, you can also make this same journey a second or third time and have it be an almost entirely new and different trip each time. With trip number one, you may find you have only enough time in your day to explore Multnomah Falls, Hood River, and Rowena Crest, leaving the Mosier Tunnels, the Maryhill Winery, and a flight in a historic biplane completely undiscovered. That means they'll all be waiting when you make your next trip!

Feel Free to Add a Day or Two

Keep in mind as you book your reservations that you can extend your road trip simply by booking a hotel reservation for two nights instead of one. This way, you'll have more time to explore the local area, hike a nearby trail, or even enjoy a drive up to majestic Timberline Lodge on Mt. Hood.

"So, Where Are You From?"

There are many blessings on a trip like this, one of which is the number of conversations you simply fall into. It usually begins with a simple question or comment, and the next thing you know, you're involved in a 30-minute conversation with some of the nicest people you've ever met. Why? Because the folks you meet on a trip like this are your neighbors, it's just that they're a quite a few houses further down the block. If you approach a town, café, museum or someone with an air of traveling arrogance, then you're making a huge mistake. Instead, be genuine and friendly. You'll be amazed at how many people you'll meet and how pleasant your trip will be.

And in those rare instances where you meet someone who loves to talk...about themselves...then excuse yourselves with the tried and true "Well, we need to be hitting the road if we're going to stay on schedule."

Get Some Good *Paper* Maps

We can't emphasize this enough. You will want to travel with and use a couple of good paper maps, and the more detailed, the better. Your phone will no doubt work well, but you're going to have the opportunity to explore some remote parts of the Columbia River Gorge, many of which have no cell signal, so your phone will not work there. In addition, your paper maps will always boot up and never run out of power.

As you make your way along and stop at various locations, you'll often see folded Oregon maps made available for free by the Oregon Department of Transportation. These are very helpful, so grab more than one and keep them with you at all times. For more detail on the roads you'll be traveling, we also recommend the large Oregon atlases put out by DeLorme. You can find them online for about $25.

Oregon's tourism division, Travel Oregon, also issues very helpful maps, magazines and trip guides. We highly recommend you visit their web site, www.TravelOregon.com, to order some of these free guides before setting out on your trip. Especially helpful is their large *Oregon Scenic Byways Official Driving Guide.*

If you are a member of AAA, check their resources, as well. By the way, make sure your membership is up-to-date.

Columbia River Gorge Parking Permits

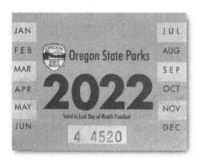

The Columbia River Gorge is bordered by the state of Washington on its northern side, and the state of Oregon on its southern side. Each state requires a parking permit for the use of some of their more popular State Parks, Trail Heads, Scenic Areas, etc. As a result, travelers will need an Oregon State Parks permit for visiting sites on the Oregon side of the Columbia River Gorge, and a Washington Parks Discover Pass for visiting sites on the Washington side. You may purchase two annual permits, one for each state, prior to leaving for your road trip, or you may purchase daily permits at the sites you visit.

Oregon State Parks Day-Use Parking Permit – Daily: $5 – Annual: $30 – This permit is honored at all 26 Oregon State Parks that charge a parking fee. Permits are available at self-service kiosks, park booths, or offices located at the site in which a permit is required. In addition, they may be purchased by calling 800-551-6949 or online at https://www.oregonstateparks.org. Note that if you purchase a *daily* parking permit at one site in Oregon, you may use that permit at any other site in Oregon that requires the same permit *for the remainder of that day.* You do not need to buy a new permit at each site.

If you decide to hike any of the trails in the Gorge, note that 10 of the more popular trails require a parking pass, and this would need to be an Annual Northwest Forest Pass, a National Forest Recreation Day Pass, or an Interagency Annual, Senior or Access Pass.

Washington Parks Discover Pass - This permit is honored at over 100 Washington State Parks and recreation sites that charge a parking fee. Permits are available at self-service kiosks, licensed vendors, or offices located at the site in which a permit is required. In addition, they may be purchased by calling 866-320-9933 or online at https://www.discoverpass.wa.gov. Note that if you purchase a *daily* parking permit at one site in Washington, you may use that permit at any other site in Washington that requires the same permit *for the remainder of that day.* You do not need to buy a new permit at each site.

Online: https://www.discoverpass.wa.gov

- 1-Day Permit: $11.50
- Annual Permit: $35.00

At the Site:

- 1-Day Permit: $10.00 Cash
- Annual Permit: $30.00
  - Via credit card if a payment kiosk is available

Convenient Tip: Located in Troutdale, at the beginning of the Historic Columbia River Highway, is a Plaid Pantry store that sells annual (not daily) Oregon State Parks Day-Use Parking Permits, thus making it convenient to stop in here before beginning your exploration of the Gorge. Located right next to the large *Troutdale – Gateway to the Gorge* sign. (Page 24) Open 24 hours a day, 365 days per year. 246 W. Historic Columbia River Highway, Troutdale, OR 97060 – 503-665-8248

Bring Some Binoculars

From dramatic waterfalls and distant volcanic peaks to circling hawks and eagles, there is much to see during your Columbia River Gorge road trip, so you may want to consider tossing in a good pair of binoculars for use throughout your journey.

8 Hours Per Day – Your Results May Vary

As we've mentioned, it's all about the journey and not the destination. That said, we found that after about 8 hours of being on the road, we were flipping this mantra and were ready to reach our destination. Our willingness to stop and explore was being replaced by a desire to simply reach our hotel, relax and "be there." Everybody's results will certainly vary, but we found that about 8 hours on the road was enough for a day.

Take Your Time and Enjoy the Sights

 As you make your way through this book, you'll see a small clock icon placed next to some of the listings. There are many Gorge attractions that do not require much time to visit. A stop at the Vista House may require about half an hour, while a stop at Rowena Crest may require half that, but locations and attractions such as Multnomah Falls, the Bonneville Dam, the Mosier Tunnels, and the Maryhill Museum absolutely call for you to spend more time enjoying the commanding views or once-in-a-lifetime experiences. Wherever you see the clock icon, plan on spending at least an hour at that location, and we would encourage you to spend even more time there while hiking to a waterfall, exploring an interpretive center, or even riding aboard a sternwheeler. If it means missing out on some of the other stops, then so be it. They'll be waiting for you on your next trip to the Columbia River Gorge!

The Historic Columbia River Highway

As you begin your journey through the Columbia River Gorge, you'll be traveling along the "King of Roads", the Historic Columbia River Highway. You will want to take a moment to read Page 134 in this guide before you begin your road trip to learn more about this scenic Oregon icon and the amazing story behind it.

We'd Love to Hear About Your Trip!

You may think that with its high quality photos, stupendous prose, and serious lack of modesty, that this book is written by a team of journalists, but nope, it's written by us, Mike and Kristy Westby. And since it's just the two of us, we'd love to hear from you about your travels, so feel free to email us a note or a photo about your trip at ContactUs@Discover-Oregon.com. We'll even send back an email in reply!

What Caused the Fire?

As you make your way along the western end of the Historic Columbia River Highway, you'll notice obvious signs of a large fire that swept through the area, as evidenced by swaths of trees with blackened trunks, chainsawed stumps, and silver tree snags covering nearby hillsides and distant ridges.

In September of 2017, a 15 year-old boy carelessly tossed a lit firework into dry grass and leaves while hiking in the Columbia River Gorge and set off a massive wildfire that burned for weeks, closed I-84 for an extended period, forced the evacuation of hundreds of people from their homes, destroyed many historic trails and structures in the Gorge, and consumed nearly 50,000 acres of forest land. Thankfully, only 15% of that area was rated as "Highly Burned".

Thanks to the brave efforts of hardworking firefighters and emergency responders, as well as countless volunteers and citizens of communities throughout the Columbia River Gorge, most of the Gorge was saved from this devastating wildfire, and today trails are being reopened, bridges are being rebuilt, and the burned areas are again springing back to life.

MAKE YOUR RESERVATIONS

The Historic Balch Hotel – Dufur, Oregon

These are the reservations you will need to make for your trip. All necessary lodging reservations are shown in bold. All other listings are optional activities.

Day 1 – Troutdale, OR to Hood River, OR

Make a reservation for 1 night

- **The Columbia Gorge Hotel – 541-386-5566**
- The Columbia Gorge Hotel Spa – 541-387-8451
- Columbia Gorge Sternwheeler - 503-224-3900

Day 2 – Explore Hood River, OR

Make a reservation for 1 night

- **The Hood River Hotel – 541-386-1900**
- Historic Biplane Flight – TacAero – 844-359-2827

Day 3 – Hood River, OR to Dufur, OR

Make a reservation for 1 night

- **The Balch Hotel – 541-467-2277**
- Tour of The Dalles Dam – Call 1 day in advance – 541-296-9778
- Nichols Art Glass - No reservation required – Just call to see if they are open today – 541-296-2143

Day 4 – Dufur, OR to Stevenson, WA

Make a reservation for 1 night

- **Skamania Lodge – 509-427-2508**

Day 5 – Stevenson, WA to Home

- Skamania Zip Lines: 509-427-0202
- Skamania Aerial Park: 509-427-0202

Day One

The Historic Columbia River Highway Scenic Byway

Troutdale to Hood River

Crown Point Vista House – Historic Columbia River Highway

DAY 1
TROUTDALE TO HOOD RIVER

Day 1 – Date: /   /

Summary: Where You're Going Today:

- Portland / Troutdale
- Historic Columbia River Highway
- Columbia River Gorge Waterfalls
- Cascade Locks, OR
- Hood River, OR

Today's route travels the Historic Columbia River Highway along the northern border of Oregon, taking you from Troutdale to the Crown Point Vista House, which offers a stunning and iconic view of the Columbia River Gorge from its western end. From there, you'll motor through history as you visit a series of graceful waterfalls on your way to the massive Bonneville Dam, where you'll witness the power of the mighty Columbia River. Afterwards, you'll explore the small town of Cascade Locks before arriving at your destination for the evening, the historic Columbia Gorge Hotel.

Tonight's Lodging:

- The Columbia Gorge Hotel & Spa

Today's Mileage: 50 Miles

Reservations Needed for This Segment:

- The Columbia Gorge Hotel – 541-386-5566
- The Columbia Gorge Hotel Spa – 541-387-8451
- Columbia River Sternwheeler – 503-224-3900

Start

Your Columbia River Gorge Road Trip begins in Troutdale, OR. To get there...

- Travel I-84 East from Portland and take Exit 17.

- Continue straight from the exit for 0.7 mile to Graham Road. Turn right here and follow this south for 0.3 mile to the Columbia River Highway / Historic Route 30. Turn left / east here, where you'll then pass under the large "Gateway to the Gorge" sign.

- You are now on the Historic Columbia River Highway Scenic Byway and beginning your road trip into the Columbia River Gorge. Note that the small

24

shops and restaurants you're passing here in Troutdale make for an excellent stop for breakfast or to grab a cup of coffee for your travels this morning.

The Columbia River Gorge

The Columbia River Gorge is a natural wonder of sublime grandeur filled with elegant and majestic waterfalls, towering geological features, endless vistas, and fields of colorful spring wildflowers that bloom from mid-February through June, and then dry in the summer winds before welcoming autumn's fiery oranges, reds and yellows.

As you travel the Historic Columbia River Highway Scenic Byway, you will pass countless waterfalls, hikes and vistas. We could include many of them here, but then that would make this a Columbia River Gorge trail guide, filling three quarters of the book. For an excellent resource on the abundance of Columbia River Gorge hiking trails and vistas, we highly recommend the book *Curious Gorge*, by Scott Cook. You'll find it in shops during your road trip.

☑ Your First Stop: Rail Depot Museum – Depot Park

Railroads have played a very important role in Oregon's history, and their history in the Gorge runs back to before the turn of the 20th century. In fact, later today in Cascade Locks, you'll see the Oregon Pony, the very first steam locomotive used in the Oregon Territory. For now, you'll visit Troutdale's Rail Depot Museum. Originally built in 1882 and rebuilt in 1907 after it burned, the museum offers visitors a look at just how the depot appeared when it was in use in the early 1900s. In addition, rail fans will find a nicely restored Union Pacific caboose in the parking lot.

Rail Depot Museum
473 E. Historic Columbia River Highway
Troutdale, OR 97060
503-661-2164

- Open: Every Friday from 10:00 a.m. to 2:00 p.m.

Driving Directions: From the "Gateway to the Gorge" sign, travel east for 0.2 miles, where you'll find the entrance to the museum on your left.

☐ Next Stop: Harlow House Museum & Park

Built in 1900, the Harlow House showcases the lifestyle, furnishings and belongings of families in the area at the turn of the 20th century.   In addition, visitors will find changing exhibits, photos, artwork, and a short interpretive pathway outside.

Harlow House Museum & Park
762 E. Historic Columbia River Highway
Troutdale, OR 97060
503-661-2164

- Open: Sunday – 1:00 p.m. to 3:00 p.m.

Driving Directions: From the Rail Depot Museum, continue along the Columbia River Highway for 0.2 miles to the Harlow House on your right.

www.Discover-Oregon.com

☐ Next Stop: Barn Exhibit Hall

The large Barn Exhibit Hall features changing exhibits which tell of the rich history of Troutdale and the surrounding area. Currently, visitors will find an impressively curated exhibit marking the 100th anniversary of the Historic Columbia River Highway, the first highway in the United States to be built as a scenic road, as well as the first to include a painted center line!

Barn Exhibit Hall
732 E. Historic Columbia River Highway
Troutdale, OR 97060
503-661-2164

- Open: Wednesday through Saturday – 10:00 a.m. to 3:00 p.m., Sunday – 1:00 p.m. to 3:00 p.m.

Driving Directions: The Barn Exhibit Hall is located next door to the Harlow House Museum & Park.

☑ Next Stop: Women's Forum Overlook

From 1912 to 1930, this spot was home to the Chanticleer Inn. Known for its famous chicken dinners, it was *the* place for the Portland elite to gather when setting out on an adventure beyond Portland. However, getting here was quite the chore, as travelers would have to journey 25 miles by train or boat to the base of the cliff below and then walk or shuttle by horse-drawn wagon up a steep dirt road to the inn. (You can find remnants of the old road as it disappears into the woods at the north end of the parking lot) Like so many buildings of this era, the Chanticleer Inn burned down, on October 8th, 1930. (Photo Circa 1916)

Today, the Women's Forum Overlook is a tribute to the founding members of the Portland Women's Forum, who worked tirelessly to raise the funds necessary to buy this point and preserve its amazing view for future generations.

Driving Directions: From the Barn Exhibit Hall, continue on the Columbia River Highway for 0.4 miles, where you'll take a right turn after crossing a large narrow bridge over the Sandy River. Continue from here for 8.3 miles to the Woman's Forum Overlook on your left.

☑ **Next Stop:** Crown Point Vista House

Offering a commanding view into the heart of the Columbia River Gorge at the west end of the old Columbia River Highway, the Crown Point Vista House is one of Oregon's classic historical icons. Built atop a massive basalt promontory in 1917, its unique stone structure is "a temple to the natural beauty of the Gorge." Inside, travelers will find a museum showcasing the history of the building and the Columbia River Gorge, as well as a small gift shop, restrooms, and a café serving coffee.

Crown Point Vista House
40700 E. Columbia River Highway
Corbett, OR 97019
503-344-1368

- Open Daily: 9:00 a.m. – 4:00 p.m.
- Closed if winds exceed 50 mph or if there is snow or ice.

Driving Directions: From the Woman's Forum Overlook, continue east on the Historic Columbia River Highway for 1.2 miles to the Crown Point Vista House.

Note that at the 0.4 mile mark you'll see East Larch Mountain Road veering off to the right, heading to Larch Mountain. This destination is not on today's journey, but if you were to come this way again and follow this road for 14 miles up to the "summit" of Larch Mountain, you'd find a large paved parking area with a path leading to a viewpoint offering an amazing "reach out and touch it" view of Mt. Hood, as well as views of Mt. Rainier, Mt. St. Helens, Mt. Adams and in the distance, Mt. Jefferson. Note that East Larch Mountain Road is closed with a gate 10 miles up the road from late fall to early spring. It is also a popular road with cyclists, so be sure to keep a careful eye out for them as you drive to the summit and back.

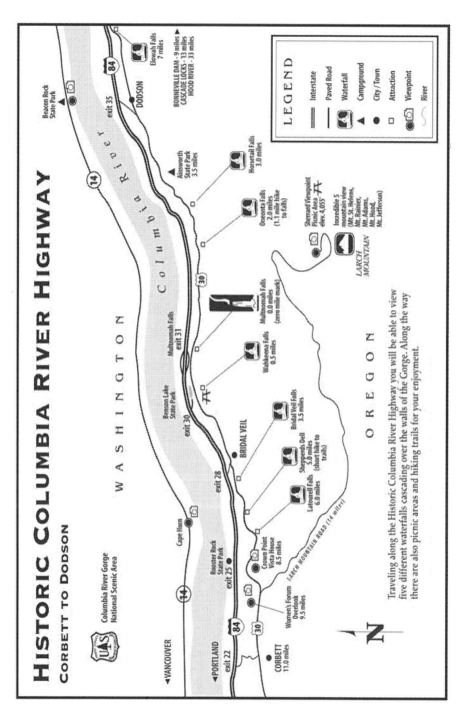

Map courtesy of Friends of Multnomah Falls

Columbia River Gorge Waterfalls

The Columbia River Gorge is home to over two dozen beautiful waterfalls close to the highway, with Multnomah Falls being by far the most popular. Appearing one after the other as you motor along, stop and visit any one of them along this stretch of the Historic Columbia River Highway. Many, such as Latourell Falls, offer short hikes with a great view.

Appearing in order as you drive east on your road trip:

- Latourell Falls
- Shepperd's Dell
- Bridal Veil Falls
- Wahkeena Falls
- Multnomah Falls
- Oneonta Falls
- Horsetail Falls

Note: Car break-ins along this stretch of the Columbia River Gorge are a chronic problem. If you stop to admire the waterfalls and do some of the short hikes, DO NOT leave valuables inside your car, nor leave bags that appear tempting within sight. Yes, you know there's nothing in that backpack, but thieves found a wallet in the last one they stole, so they'll take yours just to see what's inside. In addition, do not arrive, get out and put valuables, such as a purse or a pack, into your trunk and walk away. There is a history of thieves watching for this kind of activity so as to learn what you have and where it is stored. Because of its quick access to I-84, break-ins occur throughout this area, but especially in the Multnomah Falls and Oneonta Gorge parking lots. Don't start your trip with a broken window!

Driving Directions: Continue along the Historic Columbia River Highway and stop at any of the waterfalls along the way.

☑ **Next Stop:** Latourell Falls

Introduce yourself to the waterfalls of the Columbia River Gorge with beautiful Latourell Falls. Featuring an amphitheatre with striking columnar basalt and a distinctive yellow patch of lichen, Latourell Falls drops uninterrupted for 224 feet, often in a thin stream, before disappearing into a pool below. Follow the stairs from the parking lot, which take you up to a trail that leads to a viewpoint only a short distance away, or opt to take a slightly descending path from the west side of the parking area, near the road, to the base of the falls. Once there, cross a small foot bridge and follow the paved path only a short distance further to see an amazing example of the Arch Deck Bridge design employed by Sam Hill and Samuel Lancaster when building the Historic Columbia River Highway.

www.Discover-Oregon.com

☐ Next Stop: Shepperd's Dell Falls

Named after George Shepperd, the land owner who presented the falls and its accompanying 11 acre parcel to the City of Portland in May of 1915, Shepperd's Dell Falls drops over 90 feet in a two-tiered display before making its way under a classic 1914 deck arch bridge, a captivating example of the impressive engineering employed with the Historic Columbia River Highway. Find the beginning of the short paved path to the falls down a small flight of stairs, near the east end of the bridge.

☑ Next Stop: Bridal Veil Falls

You have your choice of two paths at Bridal Veil Falls. One leads to sweeping vistas of the Columbia River Gorge, while the other takes you to a viewing platform opposite the falls.

Make your way to the east end of the parking lot and find a trail that splits near the restrooms. The paved path to the left takes you on a short interpretive loop that leads to a collection of viewpoints high on a bluff overlooking the Columbia River. Choose the path that veers to the right, and you'll soon drop down into the forest along a gravel path that traverses a set of switchbacks, small bridges and concrete steps before leading up to a viewing platform across from Bridal Veil Falls. It's about ¼ mile, at best. Note that you'll want to be mindful of the poison oak in this area. *Photo: Megan Westby*

☑ **Next Stop:** Wahkeena Falls

A short 0.2 mile hike along a paved path takes you up to a historic hand-crafted stone bridge fronting Wahkeena Falls. Dropping as a fall and then a cascade for over 240 feet, it is one of the more photogenic falls you'll find in the Columbia River Gorge.
Note that the bridge can become heavily ice encrusted and very treacherous when temperatures reach below freezing.

☑ **Next Stop:** Multnomah Falls

As you make your way through the list of waterfalls, you'll come upon majestic Multnomah Falls. Falling in two stages, separated by the Benson Bridge, Multnomah Falls towers at 620 feet high, making it the tallest waterfall in all of Oregon and creating such an impressive site that it draws more than 2 million visitors every year. In fact, it is the most visited natural recreation site in the Pacific Northwest.

The walk from the often busy parking area to the falls is very short, and the option exists to hike up to the Benson Bridge or to continue on all the way up to a viewing platform at the crest of the upper falls for a unique and memorable view. (1.2 Miles)

Multnomah Falls Lodge, built in 1925, offers a Visitor Center, gift shop, a snack bar, and a restaurant, which serves breakfast at 8:00 a.m., lunch at 11:00 a.m., and dinner at 4:00 p.m.

- Open: Multnomah Falls is open year-round, and the Visitor Center is open daily from 9:00 a.m. to 5:00 p.m.

Driving Directions: You'll come upon Multnomah Falls as you make your way east along the Columbia River Highway.

After visiting Multnomah Falls, you'll continue to Oneonta Falls, Horsetail Falls and Elowah Falls. To do so, travel east from Multnomah Falls on the Historic Columbia River Scenic Byway for 3.6 miles to where you take the road to the right for *Hood River – I-84 – Route 30 East*. Take this and continue a little over 0.2 miles to where you turn right onto Frontage Road *instead of taking the onramp to I-84 Eastbound on the left*. (Note that it is OK if you do get onto I-84 here, you'll just miss Elowah Falls.) Continue on Frontage Road until you join I-84 just after passing the trailhead for Elowah Falls. Continue on I-84 East until taking *Exit 40 – Bonneville Dam*, in just under three miles.

☐ **Next Stop:** Oneonta Falls closed

A unique Columbia River Gorge adventure. In addition to offering hiking trails to Lower, Middle, and Upper Oneonta Falls, visitors may also climb over a large log jam and wade through Oneonta Creek up Oneonta Canyon to the base of Oneonta Falls. It's a popular hike, though most folks wait until the water level is low, since the water can be a tad cool!

Note: Due to the fire of 2017, all of the trails to Oneonta Falls, including through Oneonta Creek, are closed for an indefinite period of time.

☑ **Next Stop:** Horsetail Falls

Located right next to the Historic Columbia River Highway, graceful Horsetail Falls drops as a flowing ribbon for a full 176 feet before dispersing into a large pool at its base. Park and walk across the highway to a nearby observation area at the base of the falls. Note that the parking area on your left can come up kind of quickly, but there is a second entrance a little further along the highway.

☐ **Next Stop:** Elowah Falls

Plunging over a dramatic cliff face and free-falling for over 200 feet, Elowah Falls rewards those who make the easy 0.8 mile hike to its base with a captivating picturesque scene. A striking basalt amphitheatre offering scattered patches of bright yellow and green lichen forms the backdrop as the water falls and disperses below before disappearing amidst mossy boulders as McCord Creek.

Note: Due to the fire of 2017, the trail to Elowah Falls will be closed for safety reasons for an indefinite period.

Bonneville Lock & Dam

As you make your way deep into the Columbia River Gorge, you'll find yourself at the Bonneville Lock & Dam. Built in 1934 by the US Corps of Engineers with funding from the Works Progress Administration, the dam provided thousands of jobs for those who were out of work because of the depression. Today, in addition to providing safe passage for river vessels, it captures the mighty Columbia and harnesses its power for use in a myriad ways throughout the Pacific Northwest.

✓ **Next Stop:** Bonneville Dam Fish Viewing Window / Bonneville Lock & Dam Visitor Center

This is either a unique taste of Oregon that provides an up close look at the migrating salmon of the Columbia River, combined with an interesting lesson on the building of the Bonneville Dam...or it's a dose of disappointment mixed with history.

Much of this experience depends upon if the salmon are running or not, so it's best to call the interpretive center or the Fish Count Hotline beforehand to ask if any salmon are swimming by the viewing window during the time of your visit. Fish runs in the spring, as well as late August through October, peaking in September, provide plenty of fish to see.

- Also see the *Average Monthly Fish Count Chart* on Page 136 to see if fish may be running during your visit.
- Bonneville Dam Interpretive Center: 541-374-8820
- Fish Count Hotline: 541-374-4011

Driving Directions: Take Exit 40 from I-84 East – Turn left at the stop and proceed under I-84 onto NE Bonneville Way. Stop at the armed security checkpoint and then proceed across the locks to the large parking lot on the east side of the interpretive center. Directions to the Fish Viewing Window are clearly displayed inside the interpretive center.

Next Stop: Bonneville Dam Hatchery

Open to the public year-round, the Bonneville Dam Hatchery at the Bonneville Lock & Dam has display ponds holding thousands of trout and salmon fry, as well as sturgeon. Make your way to the small Sturgeon Viewing and Interpretive Center behind the hatchery building and step inside to see huge sturgeon and salmon swimming past the large viewing window. It is here that you'll see Herman, an adult White Sturgeon measuring more than 10' in length! Also, be sure to see the nearby Trout Pond, where the 18" trout are small in comparison to the others. Note: If you have a quarter in hand, you can buy food to feed the fish!

Bonneville Dam Hatchery
70543 NE Herman Loop
Cascade Locks, OR 97014
541-374-8393

- Exit 40 – I-84
- Located west of the Bonneville Dam

Driving Directions: Take Exit 40 from I-84 East and turn left to proceed under I-84 onto NE Bonneville Way. In a short distance, turn left onto NE Sturgeon Ln. and park near the gift shop. Then walk over to the hatchery.

If you are coming here from the Bonneville Dam Fish Viewing Window, (Page 37) look for signs to the hatchery / NE Sturgeon Ln. as you begin to leave the Dam area and approach I-84.

☐ Next Stop: Spawning Salmon (Sept. & Oct.)

During the last days of August, as well as the months of September and October, visitors to the Bonneville Lock & Dam area can see spawning salmon in nearby Tanner Creek.

Driving Directions: Exit I-84 at Exit 40, but instead of turning left and passing under I-84 to Bonneville Dam, turn right and park at the Wahclella Falls trailhead. (Which is an excellent 2-mile round trip triple-falls hike, by the way.) Walk over to the nearby Tanner Creek to see the salmon. Note that a parking permit, such as a Northwest Forest Pass, is required here.

☐ Next Stop: Cascade Salmon Hatchery

Located next to the trailhead of the popular Eagle Creek Trail is the Cascade Salmon Hatchery. Open year-round, the hatchery focuses on egg incubation and the rearing of Coho salmon, so there's a good chance you'll see its rearing ponds full of small salmon fingerlings when you stop by. Note that large adult Coho and Chinook salmon return to spawn in the nearby Eagle Creek during the months of September and October, and this can be quite the spectacle of nature to observe.

Cascade Salmon Hatchery
74152 NE Eagle Creek Loop
Cascade Locks, OR 97014
541-374-8381

- Open: 7:30 a.m. to 4:30 p.m., though visitors can walk around the rearing ponds after hours. Personnel are more than happy to answer any questions visitors may have while the hatchery is open.

Note: A parking permit is not needed when parking *at the hatchery*. If you park near the busy Eagle Creek Trail trailhead to the south, then you will need an Annual Northwest Forest Pass, a National Forest Recreation Day Pass, or an Interagency Annual, Senior or Access Pass.

Driving Directions: From the Bonneville Dam, continue east on I-84 for a little over 1 mile to *Exit 41 – Fish Hatchery – Eagle Creek Rec Area*. (Note: The exit occurs shortly after exiting a tunnel, so you may wish to be in the right lane when entering the tunnel.) The salmon hatchery is directly in front of you when you stop at the end of the exit. Do not leave valuables in your car if you park near the Eagle Creek Trailhead.

☐ Next Stop: Eagle Creek Overlook

Built in 1937 by the Civilian Conservation Corp, the Eagle Creek Overlook gave sightseers a place from which to watch the construction of the massive Bonneville Dam. Today, it gives travelers a captivating view of the dam and the river that's a little bit off the beaten path and well worth the stop.

Driving Directions: To the north of the hatchery is the onramp you will soon take for I-84 Eastbound to Cascade Locks. However, to the left of the start of the onramp is a two lane road that leads west, under I-84 and to the Eagle Creek Overlook. Take this road and follow it to the parking area, where you'll find a short trail leading north to the overlook. Note that the stretch of Eagle Creek next to the road leading west is an excellent spot to see migrating salmon during September and October.

Cascade Locks, Oregon

Located in the heart of the Columbia River Gorge, the town of Cascade Locks welcomes visitors with a growing number of restaurants, a wealth of adventures, and a fascinating story that reveals the history of the indigenous people of the area, the courage of the Oregon Trail pioneers, and the powerful geologic, hydraulic and volcanic forces that shaped the gorge.

Driving Directions: From the Cascade Salmon Hatchery and Eagle Creek Overlook, take the onramp to I-84 Eastbound and continue east to *Exit 44 – Cascade Locks – Stevenson*. This exit rolls you right onto the main drag in town, Wa Na Pa Street.

Note: When you leave Cascade Locks, you will travel over I-84 and take a backroad east, rejoining I-84 Eastbound at Exit 51.

☐ Cascade Locks Stop: Eastwind Drive-In

The place to hit after a day of adventure in the Columbia River Gorge, the Eastwind Drive-In offers burgers, fries, shakes and the largest chocolate & vanilla swirl soft-serve ice cream cone you'll ever see in your life!   Simply continue down the main drag of Cascade Locks after getting off I-84, and you'll see it on the left.

Eastwind Drive-In
395 NW Wa Na Pa Street
Cascade Locks, OR 97014
541-374-8380

☐ Cascade Locks Stop: Brigham Fish Market

If you'd prefer some delicious seafood, including halibut, shrimp, clams and oysters, as well as freshly caught Columbia River salmon and sturgeon, all prepared in a variety of ways, including Gluten Free, then stop in at one of our favorite Cascade Locks restaurants, Brigham Fish Market. Grab a table inside or enjoy outdoor seating in the sun.

Brigham Fish Market
681 Wa Na Pa Street
Cascade Locks, OR 97014
541-374-9340

Open:

- Monday and Tuesday - 11:00 a.m. to 6:00 p.m.
- Thursday through Sunday - 10:00 a.m. to 6:00 p.m.
- Closed Wednesdays

☐ **Cascade Locks Stop:** Thirsty Coffee Bar

Want to find your new favorite spot to grab a flavorful coffee, hot chocolate, iced tea, smoothie, breakfast sandwich, pastry or more when exploring the gorge? Then stop in at Thirsty Coffee Bar and enjoy their locally made offerings. Oh, and be sure to ask about The Joy Foundation.

Thirsty Coffee Bar
504 Wa Na Pa Street
Cascade Locks, OR 97014

- Open Monday through Saturday - 6:00 a.m. to 6:00 p.m., Sundays - 7:00 a.m. to 6:00 p.m.

☐ **Cascade Locks Stop:** Historical Museum

Built in 1905, the museum provides guests with a look at the history of the Cascade Locks area through displays, photos and artifacts. Outside, in its own climate controlled building, is The Oregon Pony, the first steam locomotive ever used in Oregon.

Cascade Locks Historical Museum
SW Portage Rd.
Cascade Locks, OR 97014
541-374-8535

- Open May – September - 12:00 p.m. – 5:00 p.m. - $3
- Closed Mondays, except holidays

Driving Directions: Heading east on Wa Na Pa Street, take the first left after the Eastwind Drive-In onto SW Portage Road and follow this to the Port of Cascade Locks Marine Park. Take the first left after passing underneath the railroad tracks.

☐ Cascade Locks Stop: Thunder Island

After visiting the museum, take a moment to walk across the locks, which were built over 120 years ago, in 1896, and explore the park-like setting of Thunder Island. It's an excellent way to see the locks up close, and the far shore provides a beautiful view of the river, as well as a great place to enjoy lunch from the Eastwind Drive-In or Brigham Fish Market.

Walking Directions: From the Historical Museum, walk north to the foot bridge over the locks and to Thunder Island.

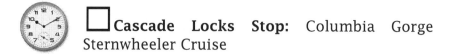 ☐ Cascade Locks Stop: Columbia Gorge Sternwheeler Cruise

See the Columbia River Gorge from "the best view on the Columbia" during a one or two hour sightseeing and interpretive cruise aboard the historic Columbia Gorge Sternwheeler. Approximately three cruises per day in the summer. Call 503-224-3900 to book your cruise.

Columbia Gorge Sternwheeler
299 SW Portage Rd.
Cascade Locks, OR 97014
541-374-8427

Driving Directions: From the Historical Museum, drive back east along SW Portage Road to the 4-way intersection by the railroad tracks, but instead of turning right to pass back underneath the tracks, proceed straight. Drive 1/8 mile to the Visitor Center and Locks Waterfront Café, located in the Cascade Locks Marine Park. Note that the Locks Waterfront Café here is open from 10:30 a.m. - 6:00 p.m. daily, May to October. 541-645-0372

☐ **Cascade Locks Stop:** Set Sail on the Columbia River

 As an option to cruising aboard the Columbia Gorge Sternwheeler, consider setting sail on the mighty Columbia! It's easy to do...simply make a reservation *at least* two hours in advance via online or by calling, meet your hosts, Preston and Chennie, at the Cascade Locks Marina, and then board their beautiful 38' sloop "Wy'East" for a two hour sailing adventure. Choose to help sail the boat or just sit back and enjoy the view. Sunset sails are also available and they are especially beautiful in this part of the gorge. By the way, the boat is a unique and very memorable wedding venue, as well.

You'll find the Wy'East docked immediately east of where you board the Columbia Gorge Sternwheeler.

Note that Wy'East holds two to six passengers. Visit their web site for additional details and to make a reservation.

Heart of the Gorge Sailing
Cascade Locks Marina
Cascade Locks, OR 97014
941-400-0050
Email: HeartoftheGorgeSailing@gmail.com
www.HeartoftheGorgeSailing.com

☐ **Cascade Locks Stop:** Sacagawea Bronze Statue

See this beautiful larger-than-life bronze statue of Sacagawea, (Sah-cog-a-way) as well as Captain Meriwether Lewis' Newfoundland dog Seaman, located outside the Visitor Center and Locks Waterfront Cafe at 299 SW Portage Rd., Cascade Locks.

To Leave Cascade Locks

Your next and last stop for the day is at the historic Columbia Gorge Hotel in Hood River. To read the directions on how to leave Cascade Locks, see the "Driving Directions" at the end of the description for The Columbia Gorge Hotel on Page 50.

☐ **Next *Look*:** Historic Broughton Flume

As you begin to approach Hood River on I-84, you'll see a large freeway sign on the right that reads *Exit 58 – Mitchell Point Overlook*. Do not take this exit, but at this point, while you're driving, look directly ahead to the opposite shore of the Columbia River and you'll spot a gray horizontal ribbon of old timbers and planks crossing a field of rocks just above the river. These boards are the remains of the historic Broughton Flume, a raised wooden flume, or channel of water, which carried rough-cut lumber from a sawmill in Willard, WA to the Broughton Mill at Hood, WA, on the bank of the Columbia River. Long since abandoned,

it is slowly decaying at the hands of time. You'll learn more about the Broughton Flume when you pass by it on the northern side of the Columbia River during Day 4 of your trip.

Photo courtesy of the History Museum of Hood River County.

TONIGHT'S LODGING
COLUMBIA GORGE HOTEL -
HOOD RIVER, OREGON

Historic Columbia Gorge Hotel - 1930s

The first day of your Columbia River Gorge road trip ends at the elegant Columbia Gorge Hotel & Spa. Built in 1921 to serve the travelers of the still new Columbia River Highway, the hotel today welcomes guests with 40 romantic guestrooms featuring views of the Columbia River or the hotel's tranquil gardens.

Guests will enjoy contemporary furnishings, including King, Queen, or Double beds, and all rooms feature a private bathroom. In addition, select rooms offer antique canopy beds and a fireplace.

And for those who wish to unwind after a day of traveling, The Spa at The Columbia Gorge Hotel offers the perfect menu of treatments to end your day. Enjoy massages, skin or body treatments, natural nail and hair services, and more. The spa is open Thursday through Monday: 10:00 a.m. to 6:00 p.m. – Other appointment times may be available. 541-387-8451 – spa@ColumbiaGorgeHotel.com

The award-winning Columbia Gorge Hotel also offers dining at its Simon's Cliff House Restaurant and Valentino Lounge, with dining on an outdoor terrace during warm summer evenings being an excellent way to finish your day.

Note: Before leaving the hotel, be sure to take the time to wander its landscaped grounds and enjoy Wah-Gwin-Gwin Falls, which falls 207 feet to the Columbia River on the north side of the hotel.

The Columbia Gorge Hotel & Spa
4000 Westcliff Drive
Hood River, OR 97031

Hotel Reservations: 541-386-5566
Spa Reservations: 541-387-8451
Reservations@ColumbiaGorgeHotel.com

- Check-in begins at 4:00 p.m.
- Check-out is at 11:00 a.m.
- Breakfast, lunch and dinner are served at Simon's Cliff House restaurant at the hotel. The hotel's famous Farmer's Breakfast brunch is available on Sundays, beginning at 10:30 a.m. The last seating is at 2:30 p.m.
- Wi-Fi is available in your room and throughout the hotel.
- Up to 2 pets (Dogs only) are welcome at the lodge. Please call 877-411-3436 to reserve a pet friendly room.
- The Columbia Gorge Hotel is a non-smoking property.

Driving Directions: From Cascade Locks...

- Drive east on Wa Na Pa Street through Cascade Locks
- Veer left onto Forest Ln.
- Follow this until it passes over I-84
- Continue over I-84 and then proceed left / east onto Frontage Rd.
- Continue on Frontage Rd. for 0.9 miles and then turn right onto Herman Creek Rd. / Wyeth Rd. Note: This is not the turnoff for the nearby Herman Creek Trailhead, which occurs at .37 miles, though both roads have the same name, "Herman Creek Rd."
- Turn left at 3.6 miles and then turn right onto I-84 Eastbound
- Follow I-84 10.8 miles east to Hood River and take *Exit 62 – W. Hood River – Westcliff Drive.*
- Turn left at the stop and then cross over I-84 and turn left again onto Westcliff Drive. You'll see the Columbia Gorge Hotel on your right. (Note: Do not take the turn for the Columbia Cliff Villas)

Lodging Option: The Hood River Hotel

Note: The Columbia Gorge Hotel is only a few miles west of Hood River. As a result, if there are no rooms available at The Columbia Gorge Hotel for this evening, then go ahead and book two nights at tomorrow night's hotel, the Hood River Hotel, which is located in "old town" Hood River. (See Page 65) Conversely, if there are no rooms available at the Hood River Hotel *tomorrow* night, then make reservations for two nights at the Columbia Gorge Hotel, beginning tonight.

Hood River Hotel
102 SW Oak Street
Hood River, OR 97031
541-386-1900

NOTES

Day Two

Explore Hood River

Mitchell Point Tunnel – Historic Columbia River Highway

DAY 2
EXPLORE HOOD RIVER

Day 2 – Date: /   /

Summary: Where You're Going Today

- Hood River, OR
- The Hood River Fruit Loop

Today you explore the busy town of Hood River, where you'll see an amazing collection of antique planes and automobiles, take to the skies in a historic biplane, walk and shop in "old town" Hood River, enjoy some hand-dipped huckleberry ice cream, travel the famous Hood River Fruit Loop, step into history at a museum or two, watch some world-class sailboarding up close, and taste your new favorite wine for the very first time, all before finishing your day at the historic Hood River Hotel.

Tonight's Lodging:

- The Hood River Hotel

Today's Mileage: 45 Miles

Reservations Needed for This Segment:

- The Hood River Hotel – 541-386-1900
- Biplane Flight – TacAero – 844-359-2827

Before You Leave:

 Be mindful of your gas level. There are numerous gas stations in Hood River, including at the south end of the bridge over the Columbia River and south of the "old town" area.

Start

Begin your day by driving to Hood River, where you'll drop right into the "old town" area. You'll explore some destinations here and on the northern end of town, close to the Columbia River, before beginning to make your way south through the Hood River Valley towards Mt. Hood, where you'll begin covering a bit more ground on the Hood River Fruit Loop. Later in the day, you'll return back to the heart of "old town" for your evening's stay at The Hood River Hotel.

Note: You may choose to have breakfast at the Columbia Gorge Hotel & Spa, or if you wish to get started on your travels, you may choose to eat at your first stop of the day, the Egg River Café. Note that this "eggceptional" cafe is very popular with locals, so you may have a wait. Maybe. If it is busy, then you'll want to try Bette's Place just down the road. See both listings on the next page. Note that there is parking for the Egg River Café in the small parking lot across the street, and the peak you see in the distance here is 12,280' Mt. Adams.

Hood River, Oregon

Home to a busy downtown area filled with recreation-minded folks, the town of Hood River is a launching point for countless outdoor adventures on the eastern end of the Columbia River Gorge National Scenic Area.

☐ Hood River Stop: Egg River Cafe

Whether you're stopping for breakfast or lunch, you'll enjoy the Egg River Café, just as all the locals do. A long menu offers your favorite breakfast items, all made with fresh local ingredients. Enjoy large portions of home-made pancakes and waffles, Egg River skillets, mixed scrambles, breakfast burritos, and even pancake, French toast or waffle sandwiches!

Egg River Café
1313 Oak Street
Hood River, OR 97031
541-386-1127

• Open: Daily – 6:00 a.m. to 2:00 p.m.

Driving Directions: From the Columbia Gorge Hotel, return east on Westcliff Drive a short distance to Cascade Avenue / Hwy 30. Turn right / south onto Cascade Avenue and follow this over I-84. Stay on this road for 1.5 miles from the hotel until you find the Egg River Café on your right, at the light.

Bette's Place

If the wait is too long at the Egg River Café, then head down the road a little ways to the "Friendliest Restaurant in Town", Bette's Place. Here you'll find a full menu of breakfast fare, as well as grandma's warm cinnamon rolls.

Bette's Place
416 Oak Street
Hood River, OR 97031
541-386-1880

- Open: Daily – 5:30 a.m. to 3:00 p.m.

Driving Directions: Bette's Place is on the corner on your left, 1 mile further east from the Egg River Café, on Oak Street.

☐ Hood River Stop: Mike's Ice Cream

As you head east down Oak Street towards "old town" Hood River, you'll pass Mike's Ice Cream on your left. It's a bit early for ice cream this morning, so Mike's isn't hopping right now, but later this afternoon and evening, especially if it is warm out, Mike's Ice Cream will be busy! Keep this location in mind if you're in the mood for some delicious hand-scooped ice cream towards the tail end of today. *Note that Mike's accepts only cash or checks.*

Mike's Ice Cream
504 Oak Street
Hood River, OR 97031
541-386-6260

- Open: Daily - April 1 to October 31 – Summer: 11:00 a.m. to 11:00 p.m. – Spring and Fall: Noon-ish to 8:00 p.m....maybe 9:00 p.m. if the day calls for it.

Driving Directions: Mike's Ice Cream is on your left, just shy of 1 mile east from the Egg River Café, on Oak Street.

□ **Hood River Stop:** Explore Hood River Shops

Oak Street in old town Hood River is home to a collection of interesting shops, stores, boutiques and more. Take some time this morning to walk the street and pop into various shops to see what you just can't live without. Along the way, you'll find bookstores, boutiques, gift shops, a surf shop, bicycle shops, sports shops, a hobby shop, a shop for your dog, and a kids shop named G Willikers Toy Shoppe. That's a lot of shops!

Driving Directions: You'll find most (but not all) of the shops in Hood River on Oak Street, east of Mike's Ice Cream. Park anywhere on Oak Street or a side street and walk.

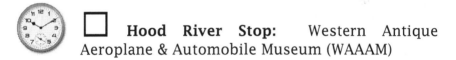 □ **Hood River Stop:** Western Antique Aeroplane & Automobile Museum (WAAAM)

Stroll among an amazing collection of over 130 flight-ready antique aeroplanes, along with over 180 intricately restored automobiles from the 1910s through 1950s, all under two large hangars spanning over 3.5 acres. In addition, visitors will find antique tractors, motorcycles, military vehicles, toys and more.

Western Antique Aeroplane & Automobile Museum
1600 Air Museum Rd.
Hood River, OR 97031
541-308-1600

- Open Daily 9:00 a.m. – 5:00 p.m. – Closed Thanksgiving Day, Christmas Day and New Years Day

- Adults: $17, Seniors & Veterans: $15, Kids 5 – 18: $8

Driving Directions: From the corner of Oak Street and North 2nd Street, proceed west on Oak Street for 0.6 miles to 13th Street. Turn left onto 13th Street and proceed 0.7 miles to where 13th Street becomes 12th Street. Continue south another 2.2 miles as 12th Street becomes Tucker Road, making a couple of 90 degree turns before reaching Air Museum Road and the Western Antique Aeroplane & Automobile Museum.

☐ Hood River Stop: Fly in a Historic Biplane

 "Discover Oregon's scenic *flyways* by day, while staying in historic hotels by night."

There is a lot to discover during your road trip, but the highlight would have to be taking to the skies and seeing the area's majestic beauty in a bright red 1942 Waco UPF-7 biplane!

 Enjoy your up-front seat for two in the open cockpit as you fly around Hood River, above the Columbia River Gorge, and even take a flight around Mt. Hood during a longer excursion. It's an amazing Oregon adventure you'll never forget! Have a group of two or three? Then make the same flight in TacAero's enclosed Cessna 172 and ride all together.

Pricing per flight – (Not per person) - Up to 2 passengers:

20 Minutes: $240 – Columbia River & Hood River
45 Minutes: $450 – Hood River valley & Mt. Hood views

Note that reservations are required, and can be made by calling 844-359-2827. Please make your reservations at least one week in advance, and note that flights may be cancelled due to the weather. At least 24 hours advance notice is requested for any flight cancellations. The combined weight of two passengers cannot exceed 310 pounds.

TacAero
3608 Airport Road
Hood River, OR 97031
844-359-2827

- Open: Year-round – Monday through Saturday – Summer: 8:00 a.m. to 6:00 p.m. – Winter: 8:00 a.m. to 4:00 p.m.

Driving Directions: From WAAAM, return to Tucker Road and turn left / west. Follow this as it turns south and in ½ mile, turn left / east onto Airport Road. You'll find TacAero at the end of the road.

 Hood River Stop: Hood River Fruit Loop & Winery Tour

The Hood River Valley is known around the world for its fruit, as well as its award-winning wines. All throughout the valley you'll find orchard after orchard of apple, pear, and cherry trees, as well as rows of grape vines, growing their delicious fruit in the perfect Oregon summertime weather. Of course, you can't have fruit without pollination, and during the month of April, all of the orchards come to life in an explosion of pink and white blossoms, which is celebrated in a number of Hood River Blossom Festival events throughout the month. If you are traveling during April, check online beginning in March at http://hoodriver.org/celebrate-blossom-time-in-hood-river/ to see this year's schedule and dates.

And when summer comes to a close, then it's time for the fall harvest, and that calls for a celebration, as well. In addition to an abundance of fresh picked fruit and fine wines being offered all along the Fruit Loop, visitors will find the annual

Hood River Valley Harvest Fest occurring for three days in mid-October down at the Event Site by the Columbia River. Visit www.HoodRiver.org/Harvest-Fest/ to learn about this year's dates, hours, and schedule of events.

Traversing all of these attractions is the 35-mile Fruit Loop. This self-guided tour visits nearly 30 different farms, wineries and vineyards offering fresh fruit, jams, jellies, syrups, fruit smoothies, ciders, baked goods, flowers, local artisan gifts, and of course, award-winning wines. Pick up a Fruit Loop map while visiting local shops in Hood River, or download one online and plan on spending a couple of hours making the tour. *Mt. Hood and Barn Photo © Peter Marbach*

☐ **Hood River Stop:** Hood River Valley Lavender Farms

Colorful and aromatic, beautiful Lavender thrives in the Oregon climate. Travelers will often find acres of its blossoms neatly aligned in rows and beckoning artists, photographers, painters, and of course honey bees and bumble bees that are attracted to its pleasing scent and bright profusion of purple color. Lavender blooms for much of the summer in Oregon, and peaks during the month of July.

Here are two Lavender Farms located in Hood River Valley, both of which are on the Hood River Fruit Loop.

Hood River Lavender Farm – Fruit Loop Stop #10

With over 70 varieties of organic Lavender, the Hood River Lavender Farm offers acres of plants blooming in the shadow of Mt. Hood. In addition to being able to cut your own bouquets, visitors will find a large variety of Lavender related items for sale, including Lavender soap, tea, perfume, oils, culinary products, aromatherapy items, dried Lavender flowers and more.

Hood River Lavender Farms
3801 Straight Hill Road
Hood River, OR 97031
541-354-9917

- Open:

  May through September - Wednesday through Saturday –
  10:00 a.m. to 5:00 p.m., Sunday 11:00 a.m. to 5:00 p.m.

  October – Friday and Saturday - 10:00 a.m. to 5:00 p.m.,
  Sunday 11:00 a.m. to 5:00 p.m.

Lavender Valley – Fruit Loop Stop #17

Visit the Lavender Farm and cut a bouquet for yourself or loved
ones, shop their farm stand for hand-crafted Lavender
products made right there on the farm, or just bring a picnic
lunch and enjoy the beautiful view of Mt. Hood.

Lavender Valley
5965 Boneboro Road
Mt. Hood Parkdale, OR 97041
541-386-1906

- Open: Late May through early September - Wednesday
  through Sunday – 10:00 a.m. to 5:00 p.m.

☐ Hood River Stop: The Hutson Museum

Located in a small building
reflecting the historic 1900
Ries-Thompson home next
door, the Hutson Museum
offers an interesting mix of
items showcasing the cultural
and natural history of the area,
including Native American
artifacts, an impressive

display of rocks and minerals, military items from WWI and WWII, and more. Admission: $1.00

The Hutson Museum
4967 Baseline Drive
Mt. Hood, OR 97041

- Open: 11:30 a.m. to 3:00 p.m. – Thursday through Sunday - April through October.

Driving Directions: While not listed on the tour map, the Hutson Museum can be found between Stops #14 and #15 on the Hood River Fruit Loop, on Baseline Drive.

☐ Hood River Stop: Apple Valley Country Store – Fruit Loop Stop #21

Huckleberries are kind of a big deal on Mt. Hood, and appearing as Stop #21 on The Fruit Loop is the Apple Valley Country Store & Bakery, which features hand-scooped huckleberry ice cream and milkshakes, as well as a wide selection of locally made items, including pies, jams, and jellies, all with fresh ingredients from local farmers. Inside, you'll find nice folks, and outside you'll find seating amongst the dahlias next to the Hood River. It's also a great place to stop at if you're cycling in the area.

Apple Valley Country Store
2363 Tucker Road
Hood River, OR 97031
541-386-1971

- Open: Wednesday through Saturday – 11:00 a.m. to 8:00 p.m.

Driving Directions: The Apple Valley Country Store is Stop #21 on the Hood River Fruit Loop.

☐ **Hood River Stop:** Watch World-Class Kiteboarders and Sailboarders

Hood River is one of the two best places in the world for kiteboarding and sailboarding, with the other being Hawaii. Visit the "Event Site" to park, get out and watch all of the action up close.

Driving Directions: From the Fruit Loop, return to the corner of Oak Street and North 2nd Street in Hood River. From here, proceed north on North 2nd Street as it crosses over I-84 and works its way down to the Event Site at the 0.4 mile mark.

☐ **Hood River Stop:** Solstice Wood Fire Cafe & Bar

If it's time for lunch or dinner, then you'll want to check out one of our favorite places, Solstice Wood Fire Cafe & Bar. Down by the Event Center and always busy, it offers pizzas and Italian fare showcasing local and Pacific Northwest ingredients, all in a fun and friendly environment with heated outdoor seating, wood burning fireplaces, and river views.

Solstice Wood Fire Cafe & Bar
501 Portway Ave.
Hood River, OR 97301
541-436-0800

* Open: Sunday through Thursday - 11:00 a.m. to 8:30 p.m., Friday and Saturday - 11:00 a.m. to 9:00 p.m. Closed on Tuesdays during the winter.

Driving Directions: From the Event Center, drive west on Portway Avenue for a few blocks and find Solstice on your left.

☐ **Hood River Stop:** History Museum of Hood River County

The Columbia River has been an important element in the history of this region for ages. With a course carved by ancient and powerful geologic forces, it has provided sustenance to Native Americans for countless generations, while its near sea-level path through the Cascade Mountain Range has attracted early explorers, pioneers, farmers, trappers, and industrialists. Visit the History Museum of Hood River County to learn of the fascinating natural, cultural, agricultural, and recreational history of this region and the Columbia River Gorge.

The History Museum of Hood River County
300 E Port Marina Dr.
Hood River, OR 97031
541-386-6772

- Open: Monday through Saturday – 11:00 a.m. to 4:00 p.m. – Closed during the month of January.

Driving Directions: From the Event Site, return to I-84 on North 2nd Street and take the onramp to I-84 Eastbound. Stay in the right lane and take the first exit, *Exit 64 – White Salmon – Government Camp.* Proceed to the end of the exit and turn left. (Onto Button Bridge Rd.) Before reaching the toll bridge over the Columbia River, turn left at the second light onto East Marina Way / East Port Marina Dr. and follow this west for 0.3 miles to the museum, on your left.

TONIGHT'S LODGING
THE HOOD RIVER HOTEL -
HOOD RIVER, OR

Built in 1911, the historic Hood River Hotel's rooms and suites welcome guests with luxurious accommodations, including European style linens, fluffy pillows and down duvets, eco-friendly spa-quality bath products, flat screen TVs, Wi-Fi, and views of the city or nearby Columbia River.

Being in the heart of "old town" Hood River, you'll be close to all kinds of cafes, coffee shops, wineries, and brew pubs. In addition, you can dine at a nearby eatery, or enjoy a meal at Broder Ost, the hotel's European inspired restaurant, before relaxing and enjoying a glass of wine in front of the wood burning fireplace in the lobby. *Hood River Hotel Photo © Ian Poellet*

- Check in: 4:00 p.m.
- Check out: 11:00 a.m.
- Pets are welcome – Inquire when making reservations

Hood River Hotel
102 SW Oak Street
Hood River, OR 97031
541-386-1900

Driving Directions: From the History Museum, return to Burton Bridge Road and turn right / south. Follow this under I-84 and then up and west, as it makes a sweeping turn south to a 4-way stop. Turn right here onto East State Street and follow this 0.4 miles to Front Street. Turn right onto Front Street and follow this around to the corner of 1st Street and Oak Street, where you'll find the Hood River Hotel on the corner on the right.

Lodging Option #1: Old Parkdale Inn B & B

Choose to stay at the Old Parkdale Inn Bed & Breakfast and you'll be treated to the warm hospitality of the owners, Steve and Mary Pellegrini. Located at the halfway point of the Mt. Hood Scenic Byway, and "this close" to Mt. Hood itself, this 1910 Craftsman home welcomes guests with three quaint rooms, each offering queen beds, luxurious beddings, flat screen TVs, private baths, free Wi-Fi and more. Better yet, right outside your door is the Hood River Fruit Loop, which you can spend all day exploring after enjoying a delicious breakfast featuring fresh fruits from the Hood River Valley. Note that the inn features an Electric Vehicle Charging Station.

Old Parkdale Inn Bed & Breakfast
4932 Baseline Drive
Parkdale, OR 97041
541-352-5551

Note: The Old Parkdale Inn B & B is located only a couple of blocks east of The Hutson Museum. (Page 61)

Lodging Option #2: Oak Street Hotel

The historic Oak Street Hotel reaches back to 1909, when it was built as a home in the early days of Hood River, before the completion of the Columbia River Highway. Beautifully restored, this award-winning hotel welcomes guests with small rooms filled with character, as well as refined amenities. Hand-forged iron queen beds, hand-crafted furniture, specially formulated bath products and more all await guests after a day of exploration. Note that while all rooms have en-suite bathrooms, some rooms have a bath separated only by a plush drapery curtain, so be sure to inquire if you wish to have more privacy during your stay.

Breakfast is served buffet style and consists of local farm fresh ingredients, freshly roasted local coffee, and tea service. A Brown Bag Breakfast to-go is also available with advance notice.

Oak Street Hotel
610 Oak Street
Hood River, OR 97031
541-386-3845

NOTES

DAY THREE

HOOD RIVER TO DUFUR

Rowena Loops – Historic Columbia River Highway

DAY 3
HOOD RIVER TO DUFUR

Day 3 – Date: /   /

Summary: Where You're Going Today

- Mosier, OR
- Rowena Crest
- The Dalles, OR
- Dufur, OR

Today you'll travel a picturesque and scenic stretch of the Columbia River Highway to the small town of Mosier and the historic Mosier Tunnels. From here, you'll motor to the captivating views of Rowena Crest before continuing on to The Dalles, where you'll explore a number of interesting sites and attractions. Your day winds up with a bit of history, as you make your way to the old Petersburg School and then your final destination for the day, (and one of our favorites) the 1907 Balch Hotel.

Tonight's Lodging:

- The Balch Hotel

Today's Mileage: 47 Miles

Reservations Needed for This Segment:

- The Balch Hotel – 541-467-2277
- Tour of The Dalles Dam – Call 1 day in advance – 541-296-9778
- Nichols Art Glass – Call to see if they are open today – 541-296-2143

Before You Leave:

If you need to get gas, you can get it down by the Hood River Bridge. Take the first exit after you get onto I-84 this morning, pass north / left under I-84, and you'll see two gas stations to the right.

Start

You'll get onto I-84 Eastbound first thing this morning before getting off the freeway 5.7 miles later at the small town of Mosier, OR. From here, you'll travel the historic Columbia River Highway into The Dalles.

To get to I-84 Eastbound from the Hood River Hotel, drive west on Oak Street for one block to the corner of Oak Street and North 2nd Street. Turn right / north onto North 2nd Street and proceed to the onramp for I-84 Eastbound.

◻ First Stop: Mosier, OR - Mosier Twin Tunnels

Closed to motorized traffic, the paved Historic Columbia River Highway State Trail takes visitors along the old Columbia River Highway to the Mosier Twin Tunnels, two impressive tunnels blasted into the basalt cliffside nearly 100 years ago. Inspired by the design of the Axenstrasse on Lake Lucerne, Switzerland, the tunnels were built with large viewing portals and observation walkways offering travelers a unique view of the gorge. Of note is the inscription carved into the rock on the north side wall at the east end of the tunnels. It reads...

Snowbound
November 19 to 27, 1921
Chas J. Sadilek
E. B Marvin

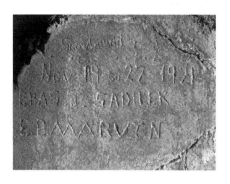

Note that there is an abundance of wildflowers growing in this area during the months of April and May, with the peak occurring in mid- to late-April.

Driving Directions: From the Hood River Hotel, proceed east on I-84 and take Exit 69 for Mosier, OR and Hwy 30. Turn right onto Hwy 30 / Historic Columbia River Highway Scenic Byway. At 0.15 miles, turn left / north onto Rock Creek Rd. and follow this 0.6 miles west to the large paved parking area on the left. Park, pay the parking fee, and then hike back down the road a short distance to the trailhead. Hike from here on the paved road 0.8 miles to the old Mosier Tunnels and viewpoint. The road is closed to cars, but open to cyclists and pedestrians, so be sure to stay to the right as you walk.

Note: While driving from Hood River to Mosier on I-84, you can spot the west entrance to the Mosier Tunnels, as well as some of the viewing windows, up on the cliffside immediately after passing the freeway sign that reads *Exit 69 - Mosier 1 Mile.*

☐ Next Stop: Mosier Plateau Trail

 A relatively short hike along Mosier Creek to the Mosier Plateau rewards hikers with a grand view, and if you're here in April and May, you'll be rewarded with colorful wildflowers, as well. Find the trail heading south at the east end of the old bridge in Mosier. Hike past Mosier Creek Falls, up four sets of stairs and switchbacks, and you're there. 3.5 Miles roundtrip, and approximately 2 miles if you hike to only the first viewpoint. Rated Moderate.

Driving Directions: From the Mosier Twin Tunnels trailhead, head back east the way you came and continue east on the Historic Columbia River Scenic Byway / Hwy 30 into Mosier. Do not return to I-84 Eastbound. As you pass through town, you'll come to a short narrow bridge. Immediately after the bridge, you'll see the trailhead for the Mosier Plateau Trail on the right. Parking for a few cars can be found on the other side of the road, but if there are no spots available here, then return back west across the bridge and park in one of the large gravel lots with a sign for the Mosier Plateau Trail.

☐ Next Stop: Route 30 Classics & Roadside Refreshments

After the Mosier Plateau hike, you're going to want some hand-scooped ice cream, so head over to Route 30 Classics & Roadside Refreshments, decide on a single or double scoop with a waffle or sugar cone, and have a seat outside as you watch folks drive and cycle by.

Driving Directions: You'll find Route 30 Classics & Roadside Refreshments on the south side of Hwy 30 as you drive through the heart of Mosier.

☐ Next Stop: Rowena Crest Viewpoint / Tom McCall Nature Preserve

This "must stop" location gives travelers a commanding view of the east end of the Columbia River Gorge, a walk among plateaus covered in wildflowers, and a high vantage point over the picturesque Rowena Loops of the old Columbia River Highway.

Note: Two short hikes may be made both above and below the parking area for Rowena Crest. The upper hike begins on the south side of the parking area and continues 1.8 miles to the summit of McCall Point. The lower trail, which begins to the west and opposite the turn into Rowena Crest, passes through wildflower meadows that bloom from late February through June, peaking in April and May. Early to mid-May offers an abundance of the brilliant yellow flowers of the Arrowleaf Balsamroot. Note that picking flowers is not permitted, and be mindful of the poison oak in this area, as well as ticks. In addition, dogs and bicycles are not allowed on these trails.

Driving Directions: Continue to follow the Historic Columbia River Highway Scenic Byway / Hwy 30 for 6.6 miles east from Mosier to Rowena Crest.

The Dalles, Oregon

Your next set of stops are in The Dalles, which showcases the ancient, rich and dramatic history of the eastern end of the Columbia River Gorge, as reflected in its archaeological sites, historical buildings, ornate Victorian and Gothic style homes, and fascinating museums.

☐ **The Dalles Stop:** Columbia Gorge Discovery Center & Museum

At over 48,000 square feet, the Columbia Gorge Discovery Center & Wasco County Historical Museum showcases a vast array of exhibits which explain the many wonders of this area, including the forces that shaped the Columbia River Gorge, the 10,000 year old culture of the gorge's native inhabitants, the journey of Lewis & Clark, and much more.

Columbia Gorge Discovery Center & Museum
5000 Discovery Drive
The Dalles, OR 97058
541-296-8600

- Admission: $9.00 – Ages 6 – 16: $5.00
- Open Daily: 9:00 a.m. – 5:00 p.m.

Driving Directions: From the Rowena Crest Viewpoint, continue down into the Rowena Loops from Rowena Crest and proceed on the Historic Columbia River Highway Scenic Byway / Highway 30 east towards The Dalles. At 7.0 miles from Rowena Crest, turn left / east onto Discovery Drive, which leads you under I-84 and back north to the Columbia Gorge Discovery Center & Museum.

☐ **The Dalles Stop:** The Dalles Riverfront Trail

Traversing the south bank of the Columbia River for 10 paved miles between The Columbia Gorge Discovery Center & Museum on its west end and (eventually) The Dalles Dam Visitor Center on its east end, The Dalles Riverfront Trail makes for a nice stroll or bike ride along the Columbia River to downtown, Riverfront Park, The Dalles Marina, and elsewhere. Find a map of the trail at The Columbia Gorge Discovery Center trailhead. Note that the first two miles of the trail leading from The Columbia Gorge Discovery Center are perhaps the most scenic.

Walking Directions: You'll find the start of The Dalles Riverfront Trail at the entrance to the parking lot for the Columbia Gorge Discovery Center & Museum.

www.Discover-Oregon.com

☐ The Dalles Stop: Klindt's Booksellers

 The next chapter of your road trip takes you to Klindt's Booksellers, the oldest bookstore in Oregon. Selling books since 1870, and from this bookstore since 1893, its shelves offer an abundance of titles, including an impressive collection of new books every month. You can even find our Oregon Road Trip books here!

Klindt's Booksellers
315 E. 2nd Street
The Dalles, OR 97058
541-296-3355

- Open Monday – Saturday: 8:00 a.m. – 6:00 p.m.
- Sunday: 11:00 a.m. – 4:00 p.m.

Driving Directions: From the Discovery Center, continue east on the Historic Columbia River Highway Scenic Byway / Highway 30 into The Dalles and stay on Hwy 30 as it automatically turns into W 6th St. (Continue straight – Do not turn left onto Webber St.) Continue on W 6th St. as it veers leftward onto W 3rd Place before joining E. 3rd Street. Follow this and then turn left / north onto Federal St. Park in street parking spots just across E. 2nd Street and walk west to Klindt's Booksellers.

☐ The Dalles Stop: City of The Dalles Fire Museum

This small self-guided museum offers a unique taste of Oregon history with its two old-fashioned steam-powered fire engines from the 1800s, as well as an interesting collection of antique fire-fighting equipment, artifacts and photos.

City of The Dalles Fire Museum
313 Court Street
The Dalles, OR 97058
541-296-5481 - xt 1119

- Located inside City Hall
- Free Admission
- Closed on Weekends
- Open Monday – Friday 8:00 a.m. – 5:00 p.m.

Walking Directions: From Klindt's, *walk* west on E 2nd Street for 1.5 blocks to Court Street. Turn left / south and walk 1 block to the City Hall building at 313 Court Street. Walk in the front door, through the hallway and down the stairs to the museum in the back.

☐ **The Dalles Stop:** National Neon Sign Museum

Located in the stately 1910 Elks Lodge in The Dalles is the National Neon Sign Museum. Here, you'll find a growing collection of colorful signs from the past, many of which you may recognize, and all arranged with interpretive displays that walk visitors through the chronological history of store front advertising, beginning with the simple reflective signs of the mid-19th century before progressing to signs lit by the new incandescent light bulb in the late 1800s, with colorful neon then following in 1910.

Be sure to make your way upstairs to walk among a collection of creative storefront facades, including Verne's Television Repair, Peggy's Beauty Shop, Chapman's Ice Cream, Medich's

Steaks & Chicken & BBQ diner, and, of course, Frank Neon Sign Co., all attracting customers with their colorful neon signs.

National Neon Sign Museum
200 East 3rd Street
The Dalles, OR 97058

- Open: Thursday through Saturday - 10:00 a.m. to 5:00 p.m.

Walking Directions: From The Dalles Fire Museum, walk to the National Neon Sign Museum, which is just across the street, on the opposite corner.

☐ The Dalles Stop: Old St. Peter's Landmark

Standing majestically over the city, the Old St. Peter's Landmark is a former Catholic Church that today serves as a beautiful historical museum. Built in 1897 with an ornate Gothic Revival architectural style, it features tall and colorful stained glass windows, a wooden Madonna carved from the keel of a sailing ship, imported Italian marble, and a towering spire which is the highest found in the Columbia River Gorge.

405 Lincoln Street
The Dalles, OR 97058
541-296-5686

- Free admission
- Tuesday - Friday: 11:00 a.m. - 3:00 p.m.
- Saturday and Sunday: 1:00 p.m. - 3:00 p.m.

Walking Directions: From the National Neon Sign Museum, walk west on E 3rd Street for three blocks to the church.

☐ The Dalles Stop: Fort Dalles Museum and Anderson Homestead

Dating back to 1905, the impressive Fort Dalles Museum is one of Oregon's two oldest history museums. Here you'll wander through a collection of original buildings from the 1856 Fort Dalles military compound, each offering a themed display of rare artifacts and items reflecting the amazing history of the area and its early pioneers. In addition, you'll find a barn filled with over 30 antique horse-drawn wagons and automobiles. Note: Be sure to ask to hear the working Edison Phonograph!

500 West 15th and Garrison
The Dalles, OR 97058
541-296-4547

- Admission: $8 – Students Ages 7 – 17: $1.00
- Open Monday – Sunday: 10:00 a.m. – 5:00 p.m. – March through November.
- Closed December, January and February.

Driving Directions: Head back to your car and, from Klindt's Booksellers, drive west on E 2nd Street for 2.5 blocks to Union Street. Turn left / south onto Union Street and proceed for 0.6 miles to E 14th Street. Turn right / west here and follow this for 4 blocks to Garrison Street. Turn left here and continue one block to the museum.

☐ The Dalles Stop: Rorick House Museum

At over 165 years old, the small Malcolm A. Moody House, home of the Rorick House Museum, is the oldest remaining house in The Dalles.

The Rorick House Museum
300 W 13th St.
The Dalles, OR 97058

- Open only during the summer months

Driving Directions: From the Fort Dalles Museum, drive north on Garrison Street for 2 blocks to W 13th Street. Turn right here and continue two blocks to the Rorick House on your right.

☐ The Dalles Stop: Nichols Art Glass

Stop in at Nichols Art Glass, grab a seat, and watch as Andy Nichols and his team practice their craft. As personable as he is skilled at the art of glassblowing, Andy will answer any questions you may have as he works to create the pieces which are displayed in galleries, private collections, and exhibits around the world. His specialty is the creation of stunning salmon and trout, each of which takes 1.5 to 2 hours to bring to life.

Want a fun new holiday tradition? Then visit Nichols Art Glass to create your own Christmas ornament. Beginning the Friday after Thanksgiving, Andy and his staff help customers design and blow their very own ornament. It's great fun for the whole family. Early reservations are strongly recommended.

Visitors to Nichols Art Glass are more than welcome, but call first to see if the shop is open and Andy or his staff will be blowing glass when you're in town. In a nutshell, Nichols Art Glass is open when it's open, so there are no set hours.

Nichols Art Glass
912 W 6th Street
The Dalles, OR 97058
541-296-2143

By the way, **Mama Jane's Pancake House** across the parking lot is very good.

Driving Directions: From the Rorick House, return west on W 13th Street for 3 blocks to Trevitt Street. Turn right / north onto Trevitt Street and follow this for 0.4 miles to W 6th Street. Turn left / west onto W 6th Street and follow this 0.2 miles to Nichols Art Glass and Mama Jane's Pancake House on your left.

☐ The Dalles Stop: The Dalles Dam Visitor Center

The massive Dalles Dam is a "powerhouse" for the region's economy. Finished in 1957, it has generated nearly 10 billion kilowatt hours of electricity, while facilitating the passage of 10 million tons of river cargo into and out of the Pacific Northwest's Inland

Empire. Stop in at The Dalles Dam Visitor Center to view interpretive displays which explain the impact of the dam from numerous perspectives, including those of the world of agriculture, power, recreation, travel, fishing, and more. Then step outside to explore the over one mile of walking trails leading to the foundations of the old Seufert Cannery and its fish wheel, as well as the historic Seufert Rose Garden, which is home to more than 90 varieties of antique roses planted by Mrs. Seufert over 100 years ago. There is no admission charge for visiting the Visitor Center.

Free tours of the dam are also offered during the summer months, and these occur at 10:00 a.m. and 2:00 p.m. beginning in early May, though times can vary depending upon the availability of personnel. *Call the Visitor Center at least one day in advance to pre-register for the tours, as space is limited.*

The Dalles Dam Visitor Center
3545 Bret Clodfelter Way
The Dalles, OR 97058
541-296-9778

- Open: 9:00 a.m. to 5:00 p.m. - Weekends from May 1 through Memorial Day, and then every day through Labor Day. Open Friday through Sundays from Labor Day until the end of September.

Driving Directions: From Nichols Art Glass, drive west on W 6th Street for 0.6 miles to the entrance to I-84 Eastbound on your right. Merge onto I-84 Eastbound and continue 3.2 miles to *Exit 87 - Dufur – Bend*. Take this exit and turn left / north onto Hwy 197 at the stop. Shortly after crossing I-84 turn right / east onto Bret Clodfelter Way and then continue for 0.8 miles to The Dalles Dam Visitor Center.

www.Discover-Oregon.com

☐ The Dalles Stop: Eagles at Westrick Park

Located north of The Dalles Dam Visitor Center, across the waterway, is Westrick Park, and every year Bald Eagles return here between mid-/late-December to mid-February to roost in the trees and feed on shad in the river below. Ten years ago, one might have hoped to see 10 eagles roosting in these trees, but today you can spot as many as 60 during the peak period in mid-January!

To see the eagles, walk north of The Dalles Dam Visitor Center, across the parking lot, to the water's edge and look in the trees across the water, in front of the large concrete wall of the dam. Note that if you didn't bring your own binoculars, you will find free stationary binoculars for viewing the eagles mounted atop posts at the Visitor Center.

Photo courtesy of Amber Tilton – US Army Corps of Engineers.

☐ The Dalles Stop: Big Jim's Drive-In

If you're getting hungry, you'll find a number of good places in The Dalles at which to eat. One place we really enjoy, especially after a day of cycling southeast of The Dalles, is Big Jim's Drive-In. It's a family style restaurant with nice folks offering sandwiches, soups, salads, hot dogs, and an amazing selection of countless hamburger choices on the menu, all made with fresh ingredients. In addition, you can choose from 16 flavors of

Oregon's Umpqua ice cream, as well as milk shakes, sundaes, banana splits, fresh fruit smoothies and more.

Big Jim's Drive-In
2938 E. 2nd Street
The Dalles, OR 97058

- Open: Daily 10:00 a.m. to 10:00 p.m. – Open to 9:00 p.m. in the winter.

☐ Next Stop: Historic Petersburg School House

A well-preserved historic one room school house that served students in The Dalles area. Note that it is not open to the public.

Historic Petersburg School
15 Mile Road
The Dalles, OR 97014

Driving Directions: From The Dalles Dam Visitor Center, return west on Bret Clodfelter Way for 0.8 miles to Highway 197. Turn left / south here and continue over I-84 to the stop at 0.4 miles. Turn right / west here and then continue 0.2 miles and take the right hand turn just past Big Jim's Drive-In that leads you to SE Frontage Road / State Road. Turn right / east onto SE Frontage Road / State Road and follow this as it turns into Fifteen Mile Road. At 3.2 miles, turn left / northeast onto what is still Fifteen Mile Road. (It's going to seem like Fifteen Mile Road continues straight, but that's now 8 Mile Road.) Drive 0.3 miles and find the school on the left.

Note: The Historic Petersburg School House is a popular starting point for many outstanding cycling routes in this area, all of which head south and east from the school. For an excellent book of cycling routes in Oregon, we highly recommend *75 Classic Rides Oregon: The Best Road Biking Routes* by Jim Moore.

A Whimsical Detour

Want to see a rafter (flock) of wild turkeys? Perhaps anywhere from 20 to 100 of them? Then leave the Petersburg School and return west on 15 Mile Road for 0.3 miles. Turn left / south onto 8 Mile road and immediately begin looking for wild turkeys in the field to your right, usually close to the tree line. If you don't see them here, continue driving a little further south on 8 Mile road, all the while looking for turkeys. You are most likely to see them within the first two miles after your turn. If you are unsuccessful, you may continue driving south on 8 Mile road, where you may spot a different rafter of wild turkeys on either side of the road anytime prior to reaching the five mile mark. Once finished, return to the Petersburg School and continue your road trip.

☐ **Next Stop:** Pathfinders Memorial

High on a road bank, clearly out of place among the wheat fields of the area, stands like a sentinel a single column of basalt. Affixed to its side is a bronze plaque, which reads... *Here lie many pathfinders to the Oregon country - Erected by The Wasco County Pioneer Association 1935.* This memorial is dedicated to those Oregon

Trail pioneers who lost their lives and were buried in a burial ground adjacent to a nearby campsite used by early pioneers on their way to Fort Dalles in The Dalles.

Driving Directions: From the Historic Petersburg School House, continue east on Fifteen Mile Road for 6.7 miles. You'll spot the lone basalt column up on the bank to the left, just to the side of the road.

TONIGHT'S LODGING
THE BALCH HOTEL -
DUFUR, OR

The historic 1907 Balch Hotel is a highlight of the trip. Josiah and Claire welcome you with homemade cookies, a refreshing drink, and a slower, genuinely friendly pace before directing you to your well-appointed period-specific room.

In addition to being your third night's stay, the award-winning Balch Hotel is also a fun weekend destination, with a lot of events occurring here throughout the year. Be sure to sign up for their email newsletter to stay in the know.

If your travel timing works out, we highly recommend you dine at the Balch Hotel this evening. Find a table under the string lights on the patio and enjoy the cool evening as you watch the sun slowly set behind Mt. Hood.

Historic Balch Hotel
40 Heimrich St.
Dufur, OR 97021
541-467-2277
www.BalchHotel.com

- Check in between 3:00 p.m. and 9:00 p.m.
- Dinner and a "delicious house made breakfast" are available – Dining reservations are required.
- To-Go breakfasts are also available with advance notice
- Ask for a room with a Mt. Hood view.
- Stock up for the next day's journey at Kramer's Market in downtown Dufur.
- The Balch Hotel does not accommodate pets.

Note: If it's warm out, then be sure to explore the landscaped grounds, complete with outdoor seating, soft shaded grass, a small pond and a patio.

If you visit Kramer's Market, be sure to walk across the street and look in the windows to see a unique Oregon sight!

Driving directions to the Balch Hotel from the Pathfinders Memorial:

From the Pathfinders Memorial, continue on Fifteen Mile Road for 3.9 miles to Kelly Cutoff Road. Turn right / west onto Kelly Cutoff Road and follow this for 2.5 miles, where you'll then turn left / south onto Emerson Loop Road. From here, proceed 5.5 miles to Ward Road. Turn left / south onto Ward Rd. and follow this 3.4 miles to Hwy 197. Turn left / south onto Hwy 197 and drive 4 miles to Dufur, OR. Take the exit to Dufur and follow the main road into the heart of town. You'll find the Historic Balch Hotel on your left at 40 Heimrich St.

Lodging Option: Victor Trevitt Guest House

Built in 1868 and recently restored with impeccable period-specific detail and antique furnishings, the historic Victor Trevitt Guest House makes for a nice alternative if the Balch Hotel is full.

The house will accommodate up to 4 guests, with 2 bedrooms, 3 beds and 1.5 baths.

Your hosts, Alan and Bev Eagy, live right next door in the historic 1867 Ben Snipes house, to the west.

Note that the Victor Trevitt Guest House is located in The Dalles, 14 miles north of Dufur.

Victor Trevitt Guest House
214 W 4th Street
The Dalles, OR
541-980-3522

Born in 1827, Victor Trevitt moved to The Dalles in 1853, and as a printer, entrepreneur, businessman, state legislator and the first judge to preside at the small Wasco County Courthouse, he played an important role in shaping the growth of this area and developing The Dalles.

www.Discover-Oregon.com

NOTES

Day Four

Dufur to Stevenson

Maryhill Museum – Columbia River Gorge

DAY 4
DUFUR, OR TO STEVENSON, WA

Day 4 – Date: / /

Summary: Where You're Going Today

- Maryhill, WA
- Horsethief Butte
- Africa?
- Lyle, WA
- Stevenson, WA

Today, you begin your journey back home on the Washington side of the river. After breakfast, you'll travel east to Biggs Junction, OR from Dufur, cross the Columbia River, and then head west, where you'll explore the interesting history of the Maryhill area, hike a geologic wonder, perhaps find an interesting antique, and actually spot a giraffe, zebra, bison and camel, all before arriving for the evening at the grand Skamania Lodge.

Tonight's Lodging:

- The Skamania Lodge

Today's Mileage: 91 Miles

Reservations Needed for This Segment:

- Skamania Lodge – 509-314-4177
- Skamania Lodge Dining Reservations - 509-427-2508
- Skamania Lodge Aerial Park Challenge Course – 509-427-0202 (Your first stop *tomorrow* morning)
- Skamania Lodge Zip Line – 509-427-0202 (Your first stop *tomorrow* morning – Call and make reservations today.)

Before You Leave:

 If you're low on gas, then be sure to fill up in Dufur, just north of The Balch Hotel. Note that the price of gas is usually pretty good at the Dufur station. Just park here and someone should come out of the General Store across the street to help you, provided you are there during business hours, which are Monday through Saturday, 8:00 a.m. to 6:00 p.m.

Start

From the Balch Hotel, return north on Hwy 197 to The Dalles and the onramp for I-84 Eastbound. From here, travel east for 17.2 miles to Exit 104. Exit here and turn left / north to cross over the Columbia River. See the Stonehenge WWI Memorial, as well as your driving directions, on Page 100 for more details.

☐ First Stop: Dufur Living History Museum

Before leaving Dufur, walk one block north from The Balch Hotel to the Dufur Living History Museum. Here, you can stroll among antique harvesting equipment, hay wagons, buckboards, an old blacksmith shop and more on the grounds outside before stepping into one of the original buildings on the site dating back to the turn of the 20th century. Inside, you'll find many impressive exhibits and displays that depict life in Oregon and the Pacific Northwest during the late 1800s to early 1900s. While you're there, be sure to ask about the story behind the bell atop the old Endersby School! The museum is free, but donations are gladly accepted.

Dufur Living History Museum
40 Main Street
Dufur, OR 97021
541-467-2205

- Open: Wednesday through Saturday – 10:00 a.m. to 5:00 p.m.

☐ Next Stop: Kramer's Market

After visiting the Dufur Living History Museum, walk over to Kramer's Market, which has been the center of Dufur for over 100 years, since 1905. Inside this old-fashioned store, you'll find a busy marketplace offering all kinds of goods, as well as local wines, a restaurant and deli, the world famous "Kramer's Sausage", and picnic tables inside and out at which to enjoy your meal. This is an excellent place to stop if you are cycling, fishing, climbing or hiking out in this part of Oregon. After you visit Kramer's, make sure you walk directly across the street to peek into the storefront windows. We won't spoil the surprise.

Kramer's Market
121 N Main Street
Dufur, OR 97021
541-467-2455

- Open: Monday through Saturday – 7:00 a.m. to 7:00 p.m., Sunday 9:00 a.m. to 5:00 p.m.

☐ Take A Look: Deschutes River Trailhead

You won't be stopping here, but we wanted to make you aware of a unique, easy, and very scenic gravel/mountain bike ride in this part of the state. On the east side of the mouth of the Deschutes River, where it flows into the Columbia River, is the Deschutes River State Park. Starting here and heading upriver is a 17 mile mountain biking trail that follows a gravel and dirt road on the east bank of the Deschutes. Traversing an old rail bed, the road/trail is mostly level and double track, as well as closed to any motorized vehicles. It's an excellent way to experience this long scenic stretch of the Deschutes River with a degree of solitude, save for the occasional train rumbling by on the opposite shore. In addition, fly fishermen in the know will bungee a fly rod to their mountain bike and head up river where other fishermen are few and far between. It's also a great overnight adventure. Just put a pack on your back, hop on your bike, and ride. Note that an Oregon State Parks parking permit is required to park at the trailhead here.

Maryhill

"The Land Where the Rain and Sunshine Meet"

Many of the attractions you see during your Columbia River Gorge road trip have a history tied to Sam Hill, the builder of the Columbia River Highway, America's first Scenic Highway, which was dedicated in June of 1916. Serving as President of the Washington State Good Roads Association, he was an active and influential proponent for the construction of good roads throughout Oregon, the northwest, and elsewhere. As part of his dreams and endeavors, he built the Maryhill Loops Road, an experimental road which he used to influence the Oregon Governor, Oswald West, and the State Legislature to allocate the funds and resources necessary for the construction of the Columbia River Highway.

After the construction of his Maryhill Loops Road, Sam Hill set out to build his home, which being grand in design, was to be the centerpiece of his Maryhill community, home to a store, post office, church, blacksmith's shop, an Inn, and acres of fruit trees. Built of thick cement, he stated *"I expect this house to be here for a thousand years after I am gone."* Unfortunately, the lack of available water in this arid climate caused his dreams of building a town to fail, and in 1917 he ceased construction on his home. In 1920, a friend of his, Loie Fuller, convinced him to finish his home and convert it into a world-class museum. Today, it is known as the Maryhill Museum, and its impressive collection includes works from around the world and features more than 80 pieces by French sculptor Auguste Rodin.

Next Stop: Stonehenge WWI Memorial

 Standing east of Maryhill, WA is a replica of England's famous Stonehenge. Built by Sam Hill and completed in 1929, thirteen years after he finished the Columbia River Highway, it serves as a memorial to the 13 young men from Klickitat County who gave their lives for our country during World War I. Nearby, you will also find a memorial dedicated to those soldiers from Klickitat County who have given their lives since that time.

Note that you'll find the tomb of Sam Hill 50 yards to the south of the Stonehenge WWI Memorial, just below a rim of basalt and overlooking the Columbia River.

Driving Directions: From the Balch Hotel, return north on Hwy 197 to The Dalles and the onramp for I-84 Eastbound. From here, travel east for 17.2 miles to Exit 104. Exit here and turn left / north to cross over the Columbia River. Soon after crossing the bridge, turn right / east towards the Maryhill State Park – Heritage Site and stay on this road for 1.1 miles until you turn left / north onto Stonehenge Drive. Follow Stonehenge Drive for 0.9 miles to the entrance to the memorial.

Next Stop: Maryhill Loops Road Overlook

Prior to the construction of the Columbia River Highway, the highway's builder, Sam Hill, and chief architect, Samuel Lancaster, built in 1911 an experimental road that snaked down a hillside towards the Columbia River, east of the Maryhill Museum. At the time, it was a masterpiece in design and execution, and its purpose was to convince the Governor of Oregon and members of the state legislature to support Sam Hill's vision for building the Columbia River Highway. Mr. Hill's idea worked as he had hoped and soon he was building *"...a great highway so that the world can realize the magnificence and grandeur of the Columbia River Gorge."*

The Maryhill Loops Road is open to non-motorized use only, and this is between the hours of 7:00 a.m. to 5:00 p.m. There is no admission fee. Access the road from its northern or southern end, off of Highway 14.

Driving Directions: From Stonehenge, turn left / north from the entrance and follow Stonehenge Drive 0.7 miles to Highway 14. Turn left / west here and follow this 1.4 miles to Highway 97 Northbound. Continue 2.3 miles north on Highway 97 to the entrance for the Maryhill Loops Road overlook on your right.

 Next Stop: Goldendale Mountain Identifier

Just north from the Maryhill Loops on Hwy 97 is the Goldendale Mountain Identifier. A large paved pullout on the west side of Hwy 97, it offers a panoramic view of the vast

Klickitat Valley as well as a rare sighting of Mt. Hood, Mt. Adams, Mt. St. Helens, and Mt. Rainier all in the same view.

Driving Directions: From the Maryhill Loops, drive north on Highway 97 for approximately 2 miles, where you'll see the pullout on your left.

  Next Stop: Lewis & Clark Overlook

An impressive observation point with interpretive signs overlooking the Columbia River immediately east of the Maryhill Museum parking area.

Lewis and Clark Overlook
57 Maryhill Museum Drive
Goldendale, WA 98620

- Open: Daily - 10:00 a.m. to 5:00 p.m.

Driving Directions: Return south on Highway 97 to the junction with Highway 14 and follow this west from here for 2.1 miles to the entrance for the Maryhill Museum / Lewis & Clark Overlook on your left.

Next Stop: Maryhill Museum of Art

Sitting on park-like grounds high above the Columbia River is the regal Maryhill Museum of Art. Built by Sam Hill and dedicated in 1926 by Queen Marie of Romania, it opened to the public in 1940 and today offers visitors an impressive collection of paintings, sculptures and furniture from around the world, including works by Auguste Rodin, as well as a beautiful display of Native American artifacts.

Admission:

- Adults: $12.00
- Seniors 65 and older: $10
- College: $9
- Youth 7 to 18: $5 (Children 6 and under are free)
- Family: $30 (2 Adults and related children 7 to 18)
- Show your receipt from any Columbia Gorge wine tasting room and receive a $2 discount off your admission.

Maryhill Museum of Art
35 Maryhill Museum Drive
Goldendale, WA 98620
509-773-3733

- Open: Daily – 10:00 a.m. to 5:00 p.m. - March 15 to November 15
- Loïe's Café – Inside the Museum – Open 10:30 a.m. to 4:30 p.m.

Walking Directions: The Maryhill Museum of Art is located next to the Lewis & Clark Overlook, to the west.

 Next Stop: Maryhill Winery

Opened in 2001, the award-winning Maryhill Winery offers its visitors a world-class collection of fine wines, all in an impressive setting high above the Columbia River. Take a seat on the patio and enjoy some of your new favorite selections while

103

enjoying the sunshine and taking in the view of 11,245' Mt. Hood in the distance. Be sure to head back this way in the future to enjoy warm evenings while listening to performers in its world-class summer concert series.

Enjoy yourself, but don't forget that you are driving today, so be sure to taste wines in moderation.

Maryhill Winery
9774 Hwy 14
Goldendale, WA 98620
509-773-1976

- Open: Daily - 10:00 a.m. to 6:00 p.m.

Driving Directions: From the Maryhill Museum, travel west on Highway 14 for 0.9 miles to the Maryhill Winery on your left.

☐ Next Stop: Horsethief Butte

As you travel west along Highway 14, you'll come upon the massive Horsethief Butte on your left. A handful of trails from the parking area will take you around the perimeter of the butte to its south side or up "into" the butte, where you can explore a maze of narrow "slots" or make your way atop the walls to enjoy the view. It's also likely that you'll find rock climbers here in the spring and fall, especially on the interior walls.

Driving Directions: From the Maryhill Winery, proceed 11.3 miles west on Highway 14 to the parking area for Horsethief Butte on your left. Note that a Discovery Pass is required for parking here, and a day pass may be purchased at the parking lot kiosk. Remember to keep an eye out for Poison oak.

☐ Next Stop: Schreiner Farms

"Am I seeing what I think I'm seeing?!"

Take a right off of Hwy 14 onto Schreiner Farms Road and instantly find yourself in Asia, Australia or Africa! You're now entering the 12,000 acre Schreiner Farms, an operating cattle ranch with over 400 cattle, as well as an amazing collection of exotic animals, including Giraffes, Wallaroos, Zebras, Camels, Bison, Ostriches, Emus, Elk, Turkeys, Geese, Antelope and many others, all wandering about in wide open areas.

Being a private ranch, all of these well cared for animals are for sale, so Schreiner Farms is not a zoo, and you cannot walk about. That said, you are more than welcome to turn up Schreiner Farms Road from Hwy 14 and travel its ½ mile length while spotting animals from your car. Heed the signs stating that you must remain in your vehicle and turn around once you've reached the Giraffe Barn. Note that the animals are most active in the early and latter parts of the day during the warm spring and summer months, or throughout the day during the cooler fall and winter months.

Since you are a guest, please be respectful of the animals, the owners, the ranch hands and any other visitors. Drive slowly and quietly, and please do not honk your horn.

Schreiner Farms
Schreiner Farms Road
Lyle, WA 98635
509-448-4580

- Usually open during daylight hours

Driving Directions: From Horsethief Butte, proceed west on Highway 14 for 4 miles to the driveway for Schreiner Farms Road, which is marked with signs. Turn right here and proceed slowly up the road to the gated area.

Note: As you approach and leave Schreiner Farms on Highway 14, keep an eye out for exotic animals roaming in the fields on the north side of the highway.

☐ **Next Stop:** Klickitat Trail - Lyle Trailhead

Beginning near the confluence of the Klickitat and Columbia rivers, in the small town of Lyle, is the Klickitat Trail. Following a former rail bed for the Spokane, Portland & Seattle Railroad, this rails to trail route winds its way for 31 miles to the grassy open plains of the Goldendale Plateau, first passing through oaks and pines along the wild and scenic Klickitat River to the town of Klickitat, WA, before following Swale Creek up into the narrow Swale Canyon and then onto the plateau.

Painstakingly restored by the diligent efforts of the Klickitat Trail Conservancy, the trail makes for a nice hike during your road trip. Park at the paved parking area and explore upriver before turning around. As an option, drive up two-lane Hwy 42 along the Klickitat River for 1.6 miles to a small turn out on your left (just before Fisher Hill Road) for a large wooden trestle. The view of the Klickitat River from the restored pedestrian friendly trestle as it flows through a narrow channel below is worth the short drive.

Note that the gravel Klickitat Trail is also an excellent mountain bike ride. Consider riding up river from the trailhead in Lyle, or drive up to the opposite end of the trail, to the trailhead off of Harm's Road, just off the Centerville Highway on the Goldendale Plateau northeast of here, and make your way downriver through open meadows before descending the slight grade into Swale Canyon, (Photo) an area rich in wildflowers and song birds in the spring. Of course, be mindful of ticks, rattlesnakes and poison oak. Though we've been on this trail many times, we've never run into rattlesnakes or ticks, but we have seen plenty of poison oak. Just keep your distance.

Driving Directions: From Schreiner Farms, continue west on Highway 14 for 6.5 miles to the western edge of the small town of Lyle. Just prior to crossing the Klickitat River, turn right onto Highway 142 North and then pull into the Klickitat Trail parking area on your left.

☐ Next Stop: Bald Eagles on the Balfour-Klickitat Loop

 During the winter months, especially mid-December through mid-February, the area around the Klickitat Trail trailhead in Lyle is an excellent location at which to spot Bald Eagles. Look for them in the trees next to the river as you make your way along the Klickitat Trail, shortly after leaving the trailhead. In addition, you can spot eagles along the nearby Balfour-Klickitat Loop trail. At .75 miles round-trip, the trail takes you to Klickitat Cove next to the Klickitat River, around which a number of Bald Eagles can be seen perched in the trees, especially when the salmon are running. Remember to bring your binoculars!

Photo courtesy of Amber Tilton – US Army Corps of Engineers.

Driving Directions: From the Klickitat Trail Trailhead, return to Highway 14 and turn right / west. Cross the Klickitat River here and then immediately turn right onto Old Hwy 8. Drive 0.2 miles and park at the trailhead for the Balfour Klickitat Park trail on your right.

☐ **Next Stop:** Catherine Creek Trail & Wildflowers

The wildflowers of Catherine Creek are some of the earliest to bloom at the eastern end of the Columbia River Gorge, with the first wildflowers of the year beginning to appear in January. Come April or May, you'll find entire hillsides covered in bright colorful flowers, including the dramatic yellow Arrowleaf Balsamroot. (Photo) The northward leading Catherine Creek trail climbs south facing slopes offering stunning views of the Gorge. 1.9 Miles round-trip with 325' of elevation gain. Note that there is also a nice mostly level paved trail on the south side of Old Highway 8 located here, which leads to benches with stunning views of the Columbia River. Caution: *Please be careful when crossing Old Highway 8!*

Driving Directions: From the Balfour Klickitat Loop parking area, turn right onto Old Highway 8 (You're not heading back to Highway 14 yet) and follow this as it curves its way west for 4.5 miles to the parking area for Catherine Creek on the north side of the road.

☐ Next Stop: Antiques & Oddities

A very popular "antiques destination" in the Gorge for more than 25 years, Antiques & Oddities is filled with an eclectic collection of quality antiques from the local area and throughout the Northwest, as well as Asia and Europe. If you stop in, be sure to head downstairs.

Full disclosure...Antiques & Oddities is owned by our very good friend, Steve Wolford, whom we've known for many years. Tell Steve we sent you.

Antiques & Oddities
211 W. Steuben St.
Bingen, WA 98605
509-493-4242

- Open: Daily - Year-round – 10:00 a.m. to 5:00 p.m.

Driving Directions: From the Catherine Creek parking lot, continue west on Old Highway 8 for 1.5 miles as it curves around Rowland Lake and meets up again with Highway 14. Turn right / west onto Highway 14 and drive another 4.6 miles into "downtown" Bingen, where you'll find Antiques & Oddities on your left.

☐ Next Look: Historic Broughton Flume

As you head to your next destination, Dog Creek Falls, you'll pass by the old Broughton Lumber Mill on your right at 4.6 miles from Bingen. Shortly after passing the mill, you'll start to see glimpses of the old wooden Broughton Flume up on the rocky hillside amidst the trees, with a good, albeit quick, view at 6.5 miles from Antiques & Oddities.

Running from Willard, WA, which is just north of here, to the Broughton Lumber Mill, the raised Broughton Flume carried rough-cut lumber, known as "Cants", down a fast moving water stream for nine miles. With a 1,000' drop along the way, the cants moved quickly, thus making the flume an efficient means by which to move the rough sawn boards to the mill, where they were processed and recut into finished lumber before being shipped out on the Spokane, Portland & Seattle Railway, (SP&S) which ran in this section of the Gorge until 1956.

The Broughton Flume was the longest and fastest water flume in the world and was in operation from 1923 to 1986, when it was abandoned. Today, you can still see fading ribbons of the old flume, and sections have been preserved in Willard, WA and at the Columbia Gorge Interpretive Center, where you'll stop tomorrow. (Page 122)

Historical photo courtesy of the History Museum of Hood River County.

☐ Next Stop: Dog Creek Falls

A short one minute hike brings you to Dog Creek Falls. Unlike the falls on the south side of the Columbia River, the 25' high cascade of Dog Creek Falls is often in the sunshine. Look for the falls to be flowing pretty good during the winter and spring months, while tapering off in the summer and fall. With such a nice reward for a short hike, this is a "must stop" during your road trip.

Driving Directions: From Antiques & Oddities, continue west on Highway 14 for 10.5 miles to a large gravel parking area on your right, behind a guardrail and just before a small sign for Dog Creek. Don't worry if you miss the parking area, because you can turn around just up ahead.

TONIGHT'S LODGING
SKAMANIA LODGE -
STEVENSON, WA

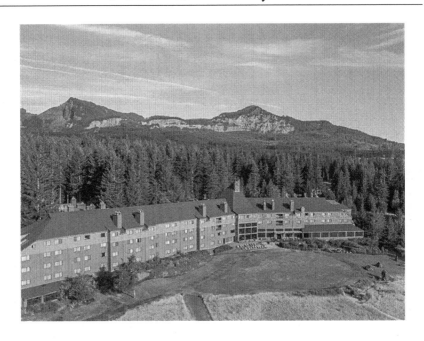

The last evening of your road trip is spent in the heart of the Columbia River Gorge at the grand Skamania Lodge. With its large timbers, warm wood paneling, Mission-style furnishings, colorful stonework, and black wrought iron accents, this 4-story Cascadian style lodge is reminiscent of the historic grand lodges of America's National Parks. Guests may relax with a book in front of the three-story stone fireplace, watch a warm

summer evening fade into night from the great lawn while taking in a sweeping view of the Columbia River, or enjoy the heated pool, the dry sauna, or indoor and outdoor whirlpools. And for true indulgence, relax after a day of exploring with a visit to the full-service Waterleaf spa. Seeking more adventure? Then enjoy the Skamania Lodge's lofty new zip line or aerial park, or take one of the three short hikes around the 18-hole par 70 golf course located amidst towering firs and a couple of large mountain ponds, each complete with basking turtles.

Retire for the evening in one of Skamania Lodge's 254 nicely appointed rooms, each of which reflect the grand essence of the lodge, or opt to stay in one of the new "Away in the Woods" Tree Houses. Set up off the ground in the forest, each sleeps up to four guests and offers a wealth of modern amenities.

Photos courtesy of Skamania Lodge

- Check-In begins at 4:00 p.m. Please call for a late arrival.
- Check-Out is at 11:00 a.m.
- Breakfast, lunch and dinner are available at one of two restaurants at the lodge; The Cascade Dining Room and River Rock. Brunch is available on Sundays.
- Dining reservations are strongly recommended and may be made by calling 509-427-2508 or online via Yelp.
- Wi-Fi is available in your room and throughout the lodge.
- Up to 2 pets are welcome during your stay.
- Skamania Lodge is a non-smoking resort.

Skamania Lodge
1131 SW Skamania Lodge Way
Stevenson, WA 98648
844-432-4748

Driving Directions: From Dog Creek Falls, drive west on Highway 14 for 12.7 miles to SW Rock Creek Drive. Turn right / north here and follow this 0.2 miles to the entrance to Skamania Lodge on your left.

Note that at the 2.0 mile mark of this 12.9 mile drive to Skamania Lodge, you'll pass the very large parking area for the Dog Mountain hike on your right. At 6.0 miles round trip with 2,800' of elevation gain, this is a bit of a stout hike, but on Memorial Day Weekend of every year, this entire parking lot overflows with cars as hikers make their way up to the top to see an abundance of wildflowers at their peak, as well as impressive views of the Gorge.

Lodging Option #1: Rivermist Lodge

A beautiful and highly rated lodge built with massive timbers, a large stone fireplace, and spacious accommodations.

Rivermist Lodge
212 Sprague Landing Road
Stevenson, Washington
98648 USA
(509) 427-4810

Lodging Option #2: The Resort at Skamania Coves

Luxurious and upscale, the homes, cottages, and condos of The Resort at Skamania Coves put you right on the river. Enjoy amazing views from your patio, or direct access to the river for sailing, windsurfing, kayaking or even fishing.

The Resort at Skamania Coves
45932 Highway 14
Stevenson, WA 98648
509-427-4900

www.Discover-Oregon.com

A Rustic
Historical Alternative

Situated at the base of a dozen towering old growth firs in the Gifford Pinchot National Forest is the historic Government Mineral Springs Guard Station. Built by the Civilian Conservation Corps in 1937 and restored in 2002, this remote cabin offers travelers privacy, an opportunity to disconnect, and an abundance of "rustic charm." Guests will find no running water or electricity, so don't plan on charging your phone and checking email. Instead, enjoy a book by a crackling fire and the light of the gas lamps after exploring the nearby old growth forest that is steep in history, as the area used to be home to a hotel, bath houses, a dance pavilion, store and gardens over 100 years ago.

Inside, guests will find a kitchen with a propane stove, gas heat, a dining area with a kitchen table, a living room with two futon couches, two bedrooms upstairs, one of which includes bunk beds, two twin beds and a nearby outhouse. (Remember, there's no running water. Think of it as camping in a cabin.)

The cabin is open year-round and is very popular in the summer. As a result, it is best to make reservations early, up to 6 months in advance. Reservations may be made online at www.Recreation.gov or by calling 877-444-6777. The key to the cabin is contained within a combination lock box by the front door, and the combination is provided with your reservation confirmation letter.

Government Mineral Springs Guard Station
2455 Hwy 141
Trout Lake, WA 98650
Ranger Station: 509-395-3400

- $65 Per Night – The Cabin sleeps up to 9 guests
- A two night minimum applies to weekend stays
- Guests must provide all food, water and supplies
- Bedding is not provided, so bring sleeping bags
- The cabin is a non-smoking facility
- No pets are allowed
- All food and garbage will need to be taken with you when you leave
- The cabin is usually snow free by early April
- When snow is present, park at the Sno-Park approximately ½ mile south of the cabin and walk, snowshoe or XC Ski in. Do not leave anything of value in your car overnight at the Sno-Park.
- All guests parking at the Sno-Park will need to have a Sno-Park permit until April 30th, and a one-day permit may be purchased for $22 at the Wind River Market in Carson, WA.

Driving Directions: From Carson, WA, drive north for 14.5 miles on Wind River Highway to the cabin. Simply drive straight without taking any turns, and you'll see the cabin on your left as the road nears its end.

NOTES

Day Five

Stevenson to Home

Beacon Rock – Columbia River Gorge

DAY 5
STEVENSON TO HOME

Day 5 – Date: /   /

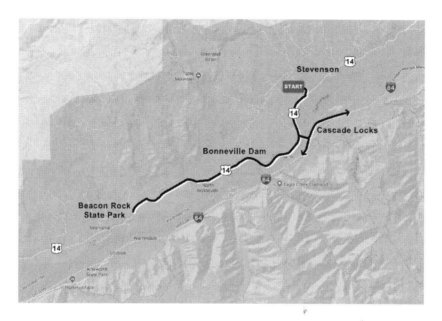

Summary: Where You're Going Today

- Skamania Lodge Aerial Park
- The Columbia Gorge Interpretive Center
- The Bonneville Dam
- Beacon Rock
- Cascade Locks, OR
- Home

Today begins with a courageous adventure...if you'd like, followed by a trip back in time to learn about the history of this area of the Gorge. From there, you'll witness the power of the Mighty Columbia before hiking a unique trail with an interesting history to the summit of Beacon Rock, all before wrapping up your Columbia River Gorge road trip adventure!

Tonight's Lodging:

- Home

Today's Mileage: 12 Miles

Reservations Needed for This Segment:

- Skamania Lodge Zip Line and Aerial Park – 509-427-0202 or visit ZipnSkamania.com
- Zip lines take flight at 10:00 a.m., 1:00 p.m. and 4:00 p.m.
- It's best to make reservations up to a week in advance during the summer season, especially for weekends.
- While visiting Beacon Rock today, you will want to *make sure* you have a Washington State Discovery Pass on your dash. You can also purchase a day pass at the site.

Before You Leave:

If you need to get gas, you can get some in Stevenson before continuing west, in North Bonneville on your way to Beacon Rock, or in Cascade Locks after crossing the bridge back into Oregon later today. Note that the bridge toll is $2.00, so you may want to have this handy when you cross.

Start

If you stayed at Skamania Lodge last night, then your first three stops of the day are close by. Simply check in for the Skamania Lodge Zip Line and Aerial Park in the conference area foyer of the lodge, and if you're visiting the nearby Columbia Gorge Interpretive Center, then you may either take a short 10 minute walk to the interpretive center from the lodge or make the brief drive.

☐ **First Stop:** Skamania Lodge Zip Line

The last day of your Columbia River Gorge road trip begins with some high-flying adventure! Take to the air on 7 different zip lines and 3 sky bridges as you make your way through a canopy of towering firs. You've never zip lined before? That's not a problem. Experienced guides will lead you through the entire course to make sure you have the time of your life!

- $99 Per person
- No age limit
- Requires approximately 2.5 hours to complete
- Zip lines take flight throughout the day – Call for times.
- Reservations are highly recommended – Call 509-427-0202 or visit www.ZipnSkamania.com - It is best to make reservations up to a week in advance, especially during summer weekends and holidays, though walk ups are sometimes available, so feel free to inquire.

Walking Directions: Check in for your adventure at the Skamania Lodge Adventures office, which may be found in the conference center foyer of Skamania Lodge.

 ☐ **Next Stop:** Skamania Lodge Aerial Park

The adventure isn't over yet! Also located at Skamania Lodge is their new Aerial Park. This lofty challenge course tests your strength, coordination, and balance as you make your way through 19 platforms and 23 elements of varying degrees in difficulty...and courage! Don't worry, however, as you're clipped in with a redundancy system, so you can never fall. While there are Park Monitors, you may guide yourself through the course at your own pace.

- $69 Per person
- Minimum 6 years of age
- Ages 6 through 8 must have a guardian at a 1:1 ratio
- Children over 8 must be able to reach up to 6 feet high
- No open toed shoes allowed
- Maximum weight limit: 275 lbs.
- Requires approximately 2.0 hours
- Reservations are highly recommended - Call 509-427-0202 or visit www.ZipnSkamania.com

Skamania Lodge Adventures
1131 Skamania Lodge Way
Stevenson, WA 98648
509-427-0202

Walking Directions: Check in for your adventure at the Skamania Lodge Adventures office, which may be found in the conference center foyer of Skamania Lodge.

☐ Next Stop: Columbia Gorge Interpretive Center

The Columbia River Gorge has been shaped by powerful geological events and fascinating cultural history for tens of thousands of years. Visit the Columbia Gorge Interpretive Center to get an understanding of these events, the history of the Gorge's first inhabitants, the Cascade Chinook Native Americans, and a more recent history reaching back only a couple hundred years. Well-curated displays convey the story behind the lives of early fur trappers, explorers, and settlers, as well as the early logging industry, the role of fishing for salmon and sturgeon, the influence of the SP&S Railroad that made its way through the Gorge, the journey of Lewis & Clark, and more.

Don't forget to see the outside exhibits and machinery, including a restored section of the old Broughton Flume, which you learned about yesterday. (Page 110)

Admission:

Adults: $10.00
Children (6 - 12): $6.00
Seniors (60+): $8.00
Students: $8.00
Family Rate (4): $30.00
Military: 10% off
AAA: 10% off

Columbia Gorge Interpretive Center
990 SW Rock Creek Drive
Stevenson, WA 98648
509-427-8211

- Open: Daily - 9:00 a.m. to 5:00 p.m.

Walking Directions: From Skamania Lodge, walk along a pathway from the great lawn to SW Rock Creek Drive. Cross here and follow the sidewalk on the other side of the road north to the Interpretive Center on your right.

Driving Directions: From Skamania Lodge, exit the lodge via SW Skamania Lodge Way and turn left / north onto SW Rock Creek Drive. Follow this 0.1 miles to the entrance for the Interpretive Center, on your right.

☐ **Next Stop:** Stevenson Waterfront Path

If beginning your day with a zip line or aerial park adventure isn't your cup of tea, then how about a pleasant and very scenic stroll next to one of the most beautiful areas of the gorge? The new Stevenson Waterfront Path winds its way along the river from Bob's Beach and the 200' pier of the Stevenson Landing to the Cascade Boat Launch half a mile to the east. Follow the paved pathway to find a bench to sit and watch the river traffic, sit on the grass to watch the sailboarders, or walk down to the river and try your hand at skipping a stone.

Driving Directions: From Skamania Lodge, exit the lodge via SW Skamania Lodge Way and turn right / south onto SW Rock Creek Drive to make your way to Hwy 14. Turn left / east onto Highway 14 and follow this for just under one mile to Stevenson. Just as you approach Stevenson, veer to the right onto 1st Street, and in two blocks turn right onto Russell Avenue. Follow this to the riverfront and park at Bob's Beach, to the right, or near Clark & Lewie's restaurant, to the left. You'll find the trail right along the river.

☐ **Next Stop:** Stevenson Farmers Market

The average vegetable travels more than 7 days and 1,500 miles before it lands on a grocer's shelf. Not with the Stevenson Farmers Market. Stop in to pick up regionally grown produce and fresh farm products sold by the actual farmers manning the booth, as well as many different items hand-crafted by local artisans. Enjoy live music, too!

- Saturdays – 10:00 a.m. to 2:00 p.m.
- Mid-June to Mid-October

Stevenson Waterfront Farmers Market
140 SW Cascade Avenue
Stevenson, WA 98648
509-427-4707

Driving Directions: Following the directions for the Stevenson Waterfront Path will take you directly to the Farmers Market.

☐ **Next Stop:** Bonneville Dam Fish Viewing Windows

If you didn't stop at the Bonneville Dam fish viewing windows while on the Oregon side of the Columbia River, then here's your opportunity to experience them on the Washington side, along with interesting exhibits on the fishing techniques and traditions of the Native Americans of the Columbia River Gorge. Note that this event is "fish dependent", so you may want to give the Visitor Center or Fish Count Hotline a call to see if fish are currently running before you stop in. Fish runs in the spring, as well as August through October, peaking in September, provide plenty of fish to see.

Washington Shore Bonneville Dam Visitor Center
Hwy 14 – Milepost 39
Stevenson, WA 98648
541-374-8820

- Open: Daily – 9:00 a.m. to 5:00 p.m.
- See the *Average Monthly Fish Count Chart* on Page 136 within this book to see if fish may be running during your visit.
- Fish Count Hotline: 541-374-4011

Driving Directions: From the Columbia Gorge Interpretive Center, return to Highway 14 and proceed west for 4.7 miles to Dam Access Road (1.2 miles *past* the dam / Visitor Center – You don't turn in at the large gate by the Visitor Center). Turn left / south here and follow this *east* 1.2 miles *back* to the dam. Stop at the guard shack and then proceed to the parking area at the Visitor Center entrance.

 ☐ **Next Stop:** Beacon Rock Hike

 Located in the heart of the Columbia River Gorge is Beacon Rock State Park. At 4,456 acres, it is home to a wealth of hiking and biking trails, but its showpiece is the massive Beacon Rock itself. Rising to 848', this former core of a volcano consists of steep faces of columnar basalt that attract rock climbers and hikers alike. Rising on its west face is a unique nearly mile-long family-friendly trail consisting of over 50 short switchbacks and countless foot bridges all leading to a summit area offering impressive views of the Columbia River Gorge. Though it climbs, the trail is not too steep, and much of it is paved and lined with handrails. Keep an eye and ear out for rock climbers who make ascents of the difficult routes on Beacon Rock's vertical south face.

Beacon Rock State Park
34841 Hwy-14
Stevenson, WA 98648
509-427-8265

Driving Directions: From the dam, return to Highway 14 and continue driving west for 3.5 miles to the parking area for Beacon Rock on your left. Be sure to display a Washington State Discover Pass or a daily parking permit on your dash here, *as this lot is patrolled often for permits.* Daily and annual parking permits may be purchased with cash or credit cards at kiosks in the parking lot for $10 and $30 respectively.

YOUR ROAD TRIP IS FINISHED!

Your Columbia River Gorge road trip is now finished! We hope you had a fun and adventurous time discovering this amazing wonder of Oregon and Washington. If you're heading home on the Oregon side of the river, you may find it most efficient to cross the Bridge of the Gods to Cascade Locks, OR. This is a toll bridge, so you'll want to have $2 available when you cross. If you're heading north to go home, then you may wish to drive west on Highway 14 to I-205 Northbound, or drive east to Highway 97 or beyond.

Thank you for choosing to use our book during your road trip, and don't forget to email us a note about your travels. You can reach us at ContactUS@Discover-Oregon.com. We'd love to hear your stories!

Mike + Kristy

Phone Numbers Oregon Road Trips - Columbia River Gorge

- Balch Hotel: 541-467-2277
- Biplane Flight – TacAero: 844-359-2827
- Bonneville Dam Interpretive Center: 541-374-8820
- Columbia Gorge Discovery Center: 541-296-8600
- Columbia Gorge Hotel: 541-386-5566
- Columbia Gorge Hotel Spa: 541-387-8451
- Columbia Gorge Interpretive Center: 509-427-8211
- Columbia River Sternwheeler: 503-224-3900
- The Dalles Dam Tour & Visitor Center: 541-296-9778
- Hood River Hotel: 541-386-1900
- Les Schwab Tire Center – Hood River: 541-386-1123
- Les Schwab Tire Center – Goldendale, WA: 509-773-5000
- Les Schwab Tire Center – The Dalles: 541-296-6134
- Lyle Hotel: 509-365-5953
- Nichols Art Glass: 541-296-2143
- Oak Street Hotel: 541-386-3845
- Oregon State Parks Parking Permit: 800-551-6949
- Rivermist Lodge: 509-427-4810
- Skamania Lodge: 509-314-4177
- Skamania Lodge Dining Reservations: 509-427-2508
- Skamania Lodge Aerial Park Reservations: 509-427-0202
- Skamania Lodge Zip Line Reservations: 509-427-0202
- The Resort at Skamania Coves: 509-427-4900
- Washington Shore Bonneville Dam Visitor Center: 541-374-8820

ADD ONE MORE NIGHT? THE 1905 LYLE HOTEL - LYLE, WA

If you'd like to add one more day to your road trip then you may wish to break up Day 4 by *inserting* a night at The Lyle Hotel in Lyle, WA. Simply book a reservation for staying here after visiting Schreiner Farms on Page 105, and then continue your journey the next morning with your first stop at the Klickitat Trail on Page 106. *If you do this, then don't forget to move your stay at The Skamania Lodge out one night. Doing this will give you another night in a unique historical hotel, and it will make for a very casual schedule on Days 4 and 5.*

The 1905 Lyle Hotel

Like much of the west, the railroads played an important role in the history of the Columbia River Gorge. Wood, wheat, grain, wool and other materials relied on the Seattle, Portland &

Spokane (SP&S) Railway to move goods shortly after the turn of the prior century, and the folks who used that railway relied upon The Lyle Hotel for a place to dine and rest.

Today, the historic Lyle Hotel welcomes travelers from around the Northwest and the world with luxurious accommodations, period-specific rooms, fine dining, and warm hospitality. You'll find all 10 of the private guestrooms on the 2nd floor, with five shared, yet still private, restrooms and baths across the hall. And for those who prefer not to hear the sound of history from the railroad tracks nearby...you'll also find a set of earplugs.

The Lyle Hotel
100 Seventh Street
Lyle, WA 98635
509-365-5953

- Check-In between 4:00 p.m. and 9:00 p.m.
- Call for early or late check-in
- Check out is at 11:00 a.m.
- The Lyle Hotel welcomes you to disconnect, so the rooms are not equipped with phones or TVs
- Free Wi-Fi is available throughout the hotel
- Dinner is served on Thursdays, Fridays and Saturdays until Memorial Day Weekend, and then Sundays are included through Labor Day Weekend
- Dinner is served at 4:00 p.m until 9:00 p.m.
- Dinner reservations are requested for parties of 5 or more
- A Continental Breakfast is available
- The Lyle Hotel is pet friendly

Want to Visit Mt. hood?

If you've never visited Mt. Hood and Timberline Lodge, but you've always wanted to, then you may wish to add a second night at the Columbia Gorge Hotel or Hood River Hotel in Hood River, OR, or the Balch Hotel in Dufur, OR, and take a day to make a trip "up to the mountain.", since you're in the neighborhood. (This will add one day to your road trip.)

One of Oregon's most famous icons, historic Timberline Lodge, set at the 6,000' timberline of Mt. Hood, welcomes visitors with a commanding presence in a lofty alpine setting, with snowy 11,245' Mt. Hood towering above to the north while the summits of the Oregon Cascades stretch far to the south. Guests are welcomed with classic 1930s-era mountain lodge architecture featuring hand-sculpted stonework, a board and batten exterior, and a massive wood beam interior featuring 70 guest rooms and showcasing a six-sided stone fireplace reaching 92' high.

Be sure to allow time to visit the museum dedicated to the construction of the lodge, which is located on the first floor, as well as to sit for a spell by the fireplace to get a sense of the ambiance and history of the lodge.

Timberline Lodge
27500 W Leg Rd.
Timberline Lodge, OR 97028
503-272-3311
www.TimberlineLodge.com

Driving Directions from the Columbia Gorge Hotel & Spa:

From the hotel, return towards I-84 and take the onramp to I-84 Eastbound. Drive east for 2.2 miles and take *Exit 64 – Mt. Hood HWY – Govt. Camp.* At the stop, turn right and follow this for 0.2 miles as the road makes a sweeping leftward curve to a 4-way stop. Proceed straight at the 4-way stop, which will put you onto Highway 35 southbound. Follow Highway 35 for 38.2 miles and then merge onto Highway 26 heading west. Continue on Highway 26 westbound for 2.4 miles to Timberline Highway, which is a two lane road. Turn right onto Timberline Highway and follow this for 5.5 miles as it climbs to Timberline Lodge.

Driving Directions from the Hood River Hotel:

From the hotel, drive east on Oak Street as it winds south for one block to E State Street. Turn left / east onto E State Street and proceed 0.4 miles to a 4-way stop. Turn right / south here onto Highway 35 and follow this southbound for 38.2 miles to where it merges onto Highway 26 westbound. Continue on Highway 26 westbound for 2.4 miles to Timberline Highway, which is a two lane road. Turn right onto Timberline Highway and follow this for 5.5 miles as it climbs to Timberline Lodge.

Driving Directions from the Balch Hotel in Dufur, OR:

From the Balch Hotel, drive south on Heimrich Street 0.2 miles to Dufur Valley Road / NF-44. Turn right / west onto Dufur Valley Road and follow this for 26.7 miles to Highway 35. Turn left / south onto Highway 35 and follow this for 12.8 miles to where you'll merge onto Highway 26 westbound. Continue on Highway 26 for 2.4 miles to Timberline Highway, which is a two lane road. Turn right here and follow this for 5.5 miles up to Timberline Lodge. Park in the large parking area below the lodge. Note: *While paved, do not drive Dufur Valley Road / NF-44 in winter or if there is snow on it.* Check with the front desk at the Balch Hotel as to if the road is currently passable.

THE HISTORIC COLUMBIA RIVER HIGHWAY

As you begin your Columbia River Gorge road trip, you will be traveling the "King of Roads", the Historic Columbia River Highway.

Built by eccentric railroad lawyer and entrepreneur Sam Hill and engineer Samuel Lancaster from 1913 to 1922, and modeled after Switzerland's Axenstrasse roadway around Lake Lucerne, the Historic Columbia River Highway stretches for nearly 75 miles from Troutdale to The Dalles, passing amidst the green maples, brightly colored moss and lush ferns of the Columbia River Gorge's western end before transitioning to the Ponderosa Pines and small oak trees dotting the semi-arid plateaus and hillsides of its eastern end. Along the way, this "great scenic boulevard", built for the Model Ts of its era, reveals a road that is an artistic masterpiece, showcasing retaining walls, guard rails, and structures master crafted from hand-hewn stone, logs and timbers. Connecting it all is a collection of graceful bridges which allow travelers to continue on their journey past stunning vistas and majestic waterfalls, with names like Latourell, Wahkeena, and Oneonta, as they make their way around, down, over and even through towering basalt cliffs toward their destination.

Though initially dedicated in 1916, the road began to pass into another era when construction on the I-84 freeway began in the 1930s. To make room for the new freeway, portions of the now "old" Columbia River Highway were blasted away, and tunnels through the basalt cliffs were either filled in or demolished. Today, however, portions of the Columbia River Highway are being restored. The Mosier Tunnels have been cleared of fill and are now open to cyclists and pedestrians, cyclists can ride from Troutdale to Cascade Locks, and the final segments of the Historic Columbia River Highway State Trail are being finished, thus allowing travelers to soon traverse from Troutdale all the way to The Dalles on the old highway or on newly restored portions closed to cars.

To learn more about Sam Hill, Samuel Lancaster, and the construction of the Historic Columbia River Highway, we highly recommend the book *Building the Columbia River Highway – They Said It Couldn't Be Done* by Peg Willis. You may want to pick up a copy and read it before you begin your journey. You'll be glad you did!

US Army Corps
of Engineers®
Portland District

AVERAGE MONTHLY
FISH COUNT AT BONNEVILLE DAM

Here are the average monthly fish counts of common adult fish that pass Bonneville Lock and Dam. These fish are unique because they are anadromous (they begin their lives in fresh water, spend part of their life in the ocean, and return to fresh water to spawn). The majority of fish migrating upstream past Bonneville do so between March and November each year. The following numbers represent the ten year monthly average from 2006-2015.

Month	CHINOOK* SALMON (KING)	SOCKEYE SALMON (BLUEBACK)	COHO* SALMON (SILVER)	STEELHEAD TROUT	SHAD	LAMPREY
January	1	0	0	543	0	0
February	3	0	0	387	0	0
March	363	0	0	1,479	0	0
April	54,569	0	0	1,361	0	0
May	116,352	84	0	1,727	240,876	787
June	79,770	193,212	0	9,502	1,907,935	5,133
July	37,564	91,374	2	87,796	113,624	10,706
August	111,089	442	10,266	154,124	272	4,386
September	429,914	13	71,599	76,994	0	1,190
October	43,332	0	46,645	10,874	0	64
November	2,117	0	5,466	1,937	0	19
December	53	0	183	779	0	1

* Jacks included

Fish climbing the fish ladder can either jump over the walls that separate pools in the ladders, or swim through holes in the walls.

DISCOVER THE
COLUMBIA RIVER GORGE

Cutting a deep gorge between Oregon and Washington, the majestic Columbia River Gorge is filled with scenic vistas, graceful waterfalls, amazing attractions, captivating history, and countless adventures, and they are all waiting for you in the *Columbia River Gorge - An Explorer's Guide.* With this guide you'll discover the many waterfalls of "Waterfall Alley", walk among the gorge's colorful spring wildflowers, fly in a vintage 2-seater biplane over Mt. Hood, see over 300 restored antique motorcars and aeroplanes up close, explore the Hood River "Fruit Loop", hike classic gorge trails, visit Oregon's oldest bookstore, discover some great new cycling roads and routes, watch world-class sailboarding, see giraffes, zebras, and camels, stay a night or two or three at one of the gorge's historic hotels, watch a master glass blower create a stunning trout out of glass, eat the biggest ice cream cone in your life, and so much more! **Over 150** things to see, do & explore!

Available Now at Retailers Throughout Oregon, Discover-Oregon.com and Online

Road Trip Oregon's Majestic Mt. Hood!

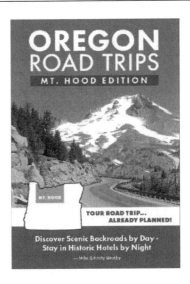

Oregon Road Trips – Mt. Hood Edition
Via the Columbia River Gorge

An alpine Oregon Road Trip adventure is waiting for you!

Set out on an exciting Oregon road trip where every night ends at a charming historic hotel, finishing with majestic Timberline Lodge at 6,000' on the south slope of Mt. Hood! Explore the Historic Columbia River Highway, hike the unique Mosier Tunnels route, visit Oregon's oldest bookstore, walk among the Columbia River Gorge's colorful spring wildflowers, fly in a vintage 2-seater biplane, ride to over 7,000' on the Magic Mile Chairlift, discover the rustic and remote 1889 Cloud Cap Inn on Mt. Hood's eastern flank, and so much more.

Available Now at Retailers Throughout Oregon, Discover-Oregon.com and Online

NOW ENJOY AN
OREGON COAST ROAD TRIP!

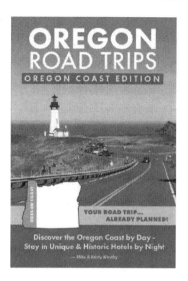

Oregon Road Trips – Oregon Coast Edition

Just as with this road trip, you'll explore the grandeur of Oregon's dramatic coastline during an adventurous 9-day road trip from Astoria south to Brookings. You'll journey along Oregon's beautiful Highway 101 as you discover countless scenic beaches, tour historic lighthouses, wander through quaint beach towns, watch whales spouting just off shore, ride in the cab of a 1925 steam locomotive, eat tasty Dungeness Crab fresh off the boat...or catch your own, stay in historic hotels, explore unique shops, meet friendly people and so much more!

Your perfect Oregon Coast road trip awaits!

Available Now at Retailers Throughout Oregon, Discover-Oregon.com and Online

DISCOVER A NORTHEAST OREGON ROAD TRIP!

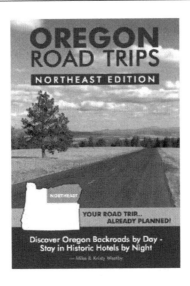

Oregon Road Trips – Northeast Edition

Just as with this road trip guide, we've already laid out an exciting 9-day journey through Northeast Oregon's scenic backroads and byways for you. Along the way, you'll ride aboard a historic steam train, wander Oregon ghost towns, ascend in a cable tram to over 8,000', stay at the Wallowa Lake Lodge, board the Sumpter Valley Dredge, explore Cottonwood Canyon, ride the rails on a 2-seater "rail car", explore unique shops, eat at great restaurants, meet friendly people and so much more!

Your perfect Northeast Oregon road trip awaits, and it's already planned for you!

Available Now at Retailers Throughout Oregon, Discover-Oregon.com and Online

AND ANOTHER GREAT ROAD TRIP IS READY!

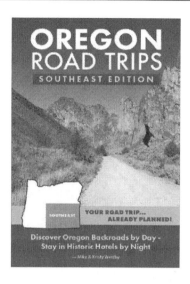

Oregon Road Trips – Southeast Edition

If you enjoyed this road trip, then you're sure to enjoy exploring remote Southeast Oregon. As with this title, you'll simply turn each page as you motor along and choose which points of interest to stop at and explore during your day's journey, *all while making your way toward that evening's lodging in a historic Oregon hotel.*

You'll drive to the top of 9,734' Steens Mountain, stay in the 1923 Frenchglen Hotel, explore the remote Leslie Gulch, see how stage coaches are built, dig for fossils, hike "Crack in the Ground", look for wild Mustangs, eat at a truly unique and remote Oregon restaurant, marvel at the geologic wonders of the Journey Through Time Scenic Byway and so much more!

Available Now at Retailers Throughout Oregon, Discover-Oregon.com and Online

SOUTHWEST OREGON AWAITS!

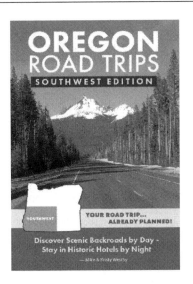

Oregon Road Trips – Southwest Edition

Visit 13 historic covered bridges, spend a night in Crater Lake Lodge, discover a vintage aircraft museum, enjoy a play in Ashland, explore deep into the Oregon Caves, wander an Oregon ghost town, see some of Oregon's most beautiful waterfalls, tour the Applegate Wine Trail, and so much more on your 9-day road trip through Southwest Oregon. As with our other Oregon Road Trip books, you'll simply motor along while you discover Oregon, and finish each night at a unique historic hotel!

Your Southwest Oregon road trip awaits, and it's already planned for you!

Available Now at Retailers Throughout Oregon, Discover-Oregon.com and Online

DISCOVER
CENTRAL OREGON

Central Oregon is a big place. To the west, high Cascade lakes and snowy peaks offer a world of alpine adventure, while to the east, the high desert beckons travelers to another world, one filled with thrilling experiences and geological wonders. In between is a land of scenic vistas, majestic waterfalls, amazing attractions, and countless outdoor and indoor adventures just waiting to be explored, and they're all here for you in the new *Central Oregon – An Explorer's Guide!* Use this guide to discover over 150 unique attractions, destinations, and experiences where you'll discover nine thundering waterfalls, set out on a moonlight kayaking adventure, walk among WWII era aircraft, hike through Oregon's high desert, ride a summer chairlift up Mt. Bachelor to enjoy some amazing alpine views, drive to the top of Paulina Peak, watch world-class rock climbing up close, paddleboard and kayak on the slow flowing Deschutes River, explore an ancient lava tube, and much more!

Available Now at Retailers Throughout Oregon, Discover-Oregon.com, and Online

WHAT TO
SEE, DO & EXPLORE
ON THE OREGON COAST!

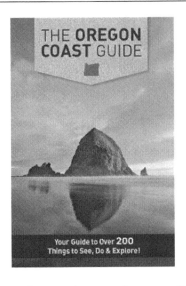

At 363 miles long, Oregon's scenic coastline is filled with countless natural wonders and attractions to see, do, and explore. Hike to a high bluff to watch for whales, walk a long sandy beach, explore a historic lighthouse, catch a live Dungeness crab, join in the fun of a sandcastle building contest, even ride aboard an old-fashioned steam train. The problem is...how do you uncover all of these activities to get the most out of your trip? The solution is the new *Oregon Coast Guide*. Inside these pages, you'll discover over 200 fun and adventurous things to see, do and explore while visiting the Oregon Coast, complete with descriptions, photos, maps, tips, a whale watching guide and much more.

Available Now at Retailers Throughout Oregon, Discover-Oregon.com and Online

ROAD TRIP
WASHINGTON'S
OLYMPIC PENINSULA

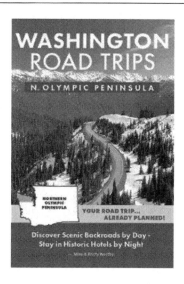

Washington's Olympic Peninsula has always been somewhat of a mystery, but now it's an adventurous and perfectly planned 6-day road trip! Set out to discover this exciting world that varies from high alpine peaks and lofty hiking trails to long sandy beaches and captivating ocean vistas. Stay at and explore the busy Victorian seaport of Port Townsend, visit a historic lighthouse, tour a vintage airplane museum, kayak on the Strait of Juan de Fuca, see majestic orcas, humpbacks, and gray whales, sleep in your very own castle, stand in the quietest place in the United States, explore unique shops, eat at great restaurants, meet friendly people, and so much more!

Your perfect Northern Olympic Peninsula road trip awaits...and it's already planned for you!

Available Now at Retailers
Throughout Washington and Online

EXPLORE WASHINGTON'S OLYMPIC PENINSULA

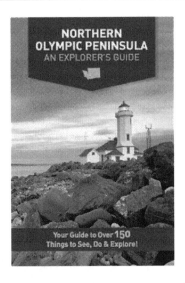

Now easily discover over 150 things to see, do and explore on Washington's Northern Olympic Peninsula!

The majestic northern Olympic Peninsula is filled with scenic vistas, beautiful beaches, graceful waterfalls, amazing attractions, and countless adventures, and they're all waiting for you in the *Northern Olympic Peninsula - An Explorer's Guide.* Tour a vintage aeroplane museum, visit historic lighthouses, learn how wooden kayaks are made, sleep in your very own castle, see Orcas, Gray Whales, and Humpbacks up close, discover the most beautiful waterfall on the Olympic Peninsula, explore historic Fort Worden, hike stunning Shi Shi and Rialto beaches, hike the captivating Hoh Rainforest, wander old town Port Townsend, and so much more!

Available Now at Retailers
Throughout Washington and Online

ABOUT THE AUTHORS

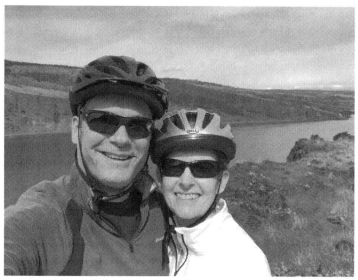

Mike & Kristy Westby – Columbia River Gorge

Having been to all six "corners" of Oregon...North, South, East, West, Top and Bottom, (The top of Mt. Hood and the Oregon Coast) we decided it would be fun to take off on a series of multi-day road trips throughout the state. During our journeys, we were surprised by the number of people we met who told us they've always wanted to do the same thing, but they never knew where to start. What routes do you take? What places do you see? How do you find them? Where do you stay? *How do you even begin?!* With that in mind, we decided to write our series of road trip guides so other like-minded travelers can easily benefit from the knowledge we've gleaned over the years and set out on their own adventures.

We'd love to hear about the journeys you've taken with our Oregon road trip guides, so feel free to drop us a note anytime or email us a photo, *especially if you're on the road!*

ContactUs@Discover-Oregon.com

WE RECOMMEND...

Building The Columbia River Highway

The intriguing story of how visionary artists, poets and engineers came together to forge a route through the mighty Columbia River Gorge and create the nation's first scenic highway, a "poem in stone." Ride along with author Peg Willis as she explores the beginnings of this miracle highway, the men who created it, and the obstacles they overcame on the road to its completion.

Peterson's Gallery and Chocolatier

Located in Baker City, Oregon is Peterson's Gallery and Chocolatier, a small shop that is part art gallery and part chocolate shop. Step past the beautiful works of locally made art and find a delectable collection of truffles, ganache, drinking chocolate, chocolate bars and more, all handmade on-site daily by Alyssa Peterson, a certified Chocolatier. Consider visiting their web site to order special Oregon made chocolates and art for your next gift. www.PetersonsGallery.net

Les Schwab Tire Centers

If you're on the road and have a flat tire, brake issues or a similar problem, we highly recommend the very helpful folks at your nearby Les Schwab Tire Center. You'll find locations in Hood River, OR, The Dalles, OR, and Goldendale, WA. Their phone numbers are listed on Page 129.

75 Classic Rides: Oregon

From an after-work ride through Portland's neighborhood streets or a family cycle along the flat Willamette Valley Scenic Bikeway, to a multi-day tour in the salty breezes of the Oregon coast— if you're seeking the best bike trails in Oregon, you'll find plenty to ride in Jim Moore's *75 Classic Rides: Oregon.*

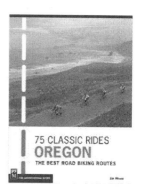

Are You a Disneyland Fan?

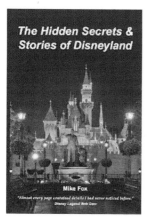

Enjoy a fascinating and entertaining book which reveals over 250 of the fun hidden secrets and story elements that the Disney Imagineers have purposely hidden for Disneyland guests to find and enjoy, complete with 225 photos!

Available online, as well as at the prestigious Walt Disney Family Museum, the Walt Disney Boyhood Home, and the Walt Disney Hometown Museum.

Want Even More Disneyland Secrets?

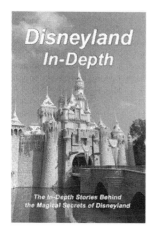

Discover the in-depth stories behind 49 magical story elements of Disneyland, *many of which are published here for the very first time.* Compiled from extensive research and lengthy interviews with Disney Legends, Imagineers, and other Disney notables.

Available online, as well as at the prestigious Walt Disney Family Museum, the Walt Disney Boyhood Home, and the Walt Disney Hometown Museum.

Are You a Walt Disney World Fan?

See and experience Walt Disney World in an entirely new way! Written by Oregon author Mike Fox, *The Hidden Secrets & Stories of Walt Disney World* reveals over 500 of the fun secret story elements that the Disney Imagineers have hidden throughout all four parks, complete with more than 400 photos.

Available online, as well as at the Walt Disney Hometown Museum and the Walt Disney Boyhood Home.

Camp Attitude

"Changing lives one camper at a time!"

Camp Attitude provides a welcoming camp experience for disabled youth and their families. Here, children with special needs can participate in all of the fun, games, excitement and interaction of a thrilling week-long "summer camp" experience, all for a nominal fee, thanks to donations from contributors who enjoy seeing a smile on a child's face...and a squirt gun in their hand!

Camp Attitude is a faith-based non-profit organization, and donations may be made by visiting their web site at www.CampAttitude.org

Camp Attitude
PO Box 2017
45829 S Santiam Hwy
Foster, OR 97345
541-401-1052

ARE YOU LOOKING TO EXPLORE BEND, OREGON?

If your explorations take you to Bend, Oregon and you'd like to rent a nice home while you're there, we'd like to recommend you consider our place. It sleeps six, is nicely furnished, and is centrally located to all kinds of fun and adventurous year-round activities. Better yet, if you contact us directly, you save having to pay the "service fees" you find when you rent a place online.

If you'd like information about our home, feel free to send Mike a note at ContactUS@Discover-Oregon.com.

NOTES

Made in the USA
Columbia, SC
04 May 2021